Windows on the Workplace

Windows on the Workplace

TECHNOLOGY, JOBS, AND THE ORGANIZATION OF OFFICE WORK

Joan Greenbaum

Second edition

Monthly Review Press
New York

Library of Congress Cataloging-in-Publication Data
    Greenbaum, Joan M., 1942-
Windows on the Workplace : Technology, Jobs, and the Organization of Office
Work / Joan Greenbaum.
    —2nd ed.
        p. cm.
    Includes bibliographical references and index.
    ISBN 1-58367-113-7 (pbk.) — ISBN 1-58367-114-5 (cloth)
    1. Office practice—Automation. 2. Employees—Effect of technological
innovations on. 3. Labor supply—Effect of technological innovations on.
4. Organizational change. I. Title.
    HF5548.G717 2004
    651.8—dc22
    2004017814

Monthly Review Press
122 West 27th Street
New York, NY 10001

Designed and typeset by Terry J. Allen, New York, NY
Printed in Canada

CONTENTS

To Harriet and Nathan Greenbaum
who taught me
to read between the lines.

Preface

In 1966 I moved to New York and landed a job as a programmer at IBM. Getting a job as a programmer at that time generally required some college (I had a bachelor's degree in economics), some luck with a thing called the Programmer Aptitude Test (I worked with a placement agency that taught me how to take the test) and what someone called "passing the mirror test" (if they held a mirror to your nose and it fogged up, you were hired). This situation was quite different from that of the 1970s through the 1990s when programming jobs and competition for the jobs were growing. And it is markedly different from the situation today as programming work has begun to follow the path of so many other jobs that are being outsourced from the countries that used to do them.

I worked as a programmer, analyst, project manager, and consultant up through the early 1970s, when, in an attempt to figure out how computers were being used to affect jobs, I went to graduate school to study political economy. Then, as now, popular accounts of technology surrounded us with the belief that computers would bring more highly skilled and better jobs. The myth was in the making that a high-tech world would create highly skilled work. I itched to use my knowledge about how computer systems were designed to peel away the high-tech glitter surrounding such critical issues.

Today we are constantly told a continuation of this tale which takes the form that the Internet will generate new high-tech jobs by creating new services in a new economy. But as the stories, examples, and data in this book will show, white-collar jobs—the backbone of the so-called information society or new economy, and a key pillar of what popular media call the "knowledge economy"—are not showing any strong growth trends, certainly not enough to absorb those workers "displaced" from other jobs. At least not workers displaced within their own countries. And job growth, such as it is, seems to be not so much rooted in the traditional notion of a job, but in the flexibility of a worker to find what the U. S. Bureau of Labor Statistics calls "alternative work arrangements."

This situation is not without historical precedent. In the second half of the nineteenth century, work and workers were moved from small farms and shops and placed in increasingly large and centralized factories that were owned not by individuals but by corporations. Steam-powered factories and railroads and steamships and telegraphs were introduced into this pressure cooker of emerging industrial capitalism in order to speed up work, cut time, and increase productivity. Technology was held up as a model of "progress and advancement," and icons like drawings of smokestacks and telegraph machines appeared in everything from American art and literature to newspapers and trade exhibitions. This grandiose faith in technology and its forward advance toward a better society was even more pronounced in the United States than in other industrialized nations, taking on what some thought of as almost religious significance.[1]

As we stand in the twenty-first century being bombarded with phrases like "thanks to advances in technology..." or "with the advent of computers…," it is almost as if we are expected to believe that technology comes along with an inevitable force—a sort of technological leap of faith. Instead, we need to reshape the debate in order to have a clear picture of the world around us. Young people who are entering the job market and more experienced workers trying to find new jobs and careers too often find themselves surrounded by an older generation telling them things like "Technology is the wave of the future," often urging them to go to school to learn "computers" or some such simple solution. Such advice, while generally offered with concern, unfortunately is still stuck in the nineteenth- and twentieth-century myths that surround the design and use of technology.

This book tackles these myths and lays out a more complex and interactive picture—putting people back into the driver's seat of change by telling stories about what is happening to jobs and what is happening when technologies are designed, produced, and then used in real work situations.

Optimistic and shortsighted views about technology driving workplace change lead to wrong-headed solutions. For example, while mainstream popular attention is directed toward high-tech/high-skill scenarios, such a focus leads to policies that encourage narrowly defined job training or training in so-called computer literacy skills. Nothing could be further from what is actually needed.

To debunk the myth of technological determinism we need to look more closely at work and the organization and meaning of work and jobs. For most of the twentieth century, office work and workplace social activities have carried meanings beyond the obvious need for income. Particularly in America, the work ethic drives the culture so completely that "What do you do?" is a form of social greeting. Work means a place to go. It may also mean a social group, a clique of friends or colleagues to talk to. Many people identify to some degree with their work; they want to do a good job and feel good about it. By taking pride in work, they come away with a sense of self-respect. And many people, in trying to work to their potential, have invested something of themselves in education, training, and on-the-job experience.

The social and financial importance of work remains the same for people, but jobs are changing. There is less security in having a job now than there was a decade ago. More and more jobs are temporary or contracted out for short periods of time. Competition for jobs increases as more and more people complete more years of schooling and the number of full-time jobs that match their specific qualifications decreases. And for so many people, particularly younger workers, the number of hours they work has increased so much that the line between work life and home life has become blurred. Many people think it is only happening to them. At kitchen tables, in living rooms, or out at social gatherings, they talk tentatively about how they seem to be having trouble finding a good job—one like the job they used to have or want to get. There is much talk about how their company may have "downsized" them, or how a particular manager was too stupid to stop the moves that the company was making, or how their company unfortunately got stuck in a bad market or bad merger. Recent high school and college graduates wonder whether there would be more job opportunities if they had only studied something different or perhaps lived in a different place.

These people are not alone. The changes being made to jobs are affecting a wide range of workers, from recent graduates to those being pushed toward early retirement. During the feminist movement of the 1960s and 1970s, we used to say that the "personal is political." This expression clearly applies to the workforce: what people are experiencing as a personal problem is a deeply rooted and broad-ranging political one. There is a whole lot of blaming-the-victim going on, and this is effective in isolating people rather than allowing them to come forward and find out what they can do together. Even the creation of terms like "computer illiterate" makes people believe that it is somehow their fault that they have been left out of the televised version of a high-tech society. Yet it is no more possible to be computer illiterate than it is to be telephone illiterate, for using computer applications, like using telephones, depends mainly on knowing the task that you are doing. Once you know the task, pushing the right buttons follows.

This book is written as a path away from high-tech glitter and toward a place where we can find ways to analyze change in order to make better choices. Since changes in work and new technology are most often lumped under the theme of "technical change," this book tries to pull that apart by explaining how decisions are made to bring about both technical and organizational restructuring. Here you will find research, stories, examples, statistics, and historical analysis that will help us look more clearly out of windows that are not clouded by overly optimistic and misleading visions. A central theme running though the book is the way that skills get redefined and reshaped, essentially to lower salaries and to cut up work so that pieces of it can be programmed into software and databases. By deconstructing the high-tech myths, I am also setting them within a macro or broader economic understanding of how and why these changes are coming about.

Four themes will be developed and illustrated through examples as the chapters of the book unfold:

1. Management reorganizes work *before* new technology is introduced. This is accomplished, in part, by analyzing work and cutting it up into specific tasks (like repeated scripts in call centers). These smaller units of work then can be more clearly specified and coded into software and databases (rationalization of work).

2. People applying for jobs are expected to have more skills, and more experience; however, these skills (including programming and web design) are often devalued in order to rein in salaries. (lowering wages).

3. Organizations and consultants reorganize work, through both specialization and integration of the work tasks that they divided up in the first place, so that fewer people can do more work (increasing productivity).

4. Companies and government agencies are increasingly carving up services into smaller units (as they do with work tasks) so that these services (such as insurance policies) can be sold as products on the Web, on the phone, and anywhere in the world (commoditization of services).

In addition to explaining these changes, this book is also about analysis and taking action. If we use analytical tools to dig more deeply into issues, we will be able to choose alternative courses of action. Looking optimistically toward the future, as proponents of a "high-tech world" would ask us to, doesn't help us learn from the past. And looking pessimistically at the mistakes and misdeeds of large corporations holds us back from taking positive action. If we are going to create paths to alternative futures and shape realistic social and economic choices, we need to move beyond the talkshow version of contemporary life. Social choice, including technological choice, can take many forms. It can come in almost any shape, including community group programs, workplace associations, professional groups, unions, and governmental legislation, as well as direct actions like those occurring around the world when officials of the World Trade Organization (WTO) meet. Whatever we choose to accomplish and change requires more than a technological leap of faith.

When I began research on the first edition of this book in 1993, the terms office work and white-collar work were generally used to define jobs that were done *inside offices* for individual employers like large corporations. Most white-collar work was also to be found inside of *occupational groups* with job categories such as accountant, bookkeeper, computer programmer, purchasing manager, librarian, and the like. Now, a decade later, workplaces can be found in homes, in cars, on mobile phones, in airport lounges, and in a variety of settings. And most workers are learning that they need to jump from job to job and be prepared to be self-employed. Not insignificantly, while government agencies still keep data on traditional occupational categories, most people entering the labor market are finding out that they should not focus on a set of skills for a specific occupation or career. Workers at all levels and in all types of work arrangements find, sort, arrange, analyze, and use information in similar ways, regardless of their occupational classification. Flexibility—in work, workers, job titles, occupational categories, work arrangements, working time, and workplaces—is the name of the game.

The data and examples in the book are largely drawn from U. S. workplaces and statistics. I conducted over fifty in-depth interviews, with the majority situated inside of people's workplaces. Since the focus of the interviews was on what people actually do in their jobs, it was important to situate their activities inside of their working environment.[2] This helped me visualize the complexities of their work and let me ask questions about the particular hardware, software, and procedures they used. Of course, when the workers felt that my presence would cause problems, some interviews were done in homes and coffee shops outside of work environments.

There were many people who helped me make sense out of the world in putting together the earlier edition of this book. I thank: Tone Bratteteig, Sheila Crowell, Ellen Kolba, Lucy Suchman, Susan Leigh Star, Sharon Szymanski, and Bill Tabb. That edition was marvelously managed through editing by Susan Lowe and Renee Pendergrass of Monthly Review Press. In particular I owe a tremendous debt to the memory of Paul Sweezy, who in reviewing a paper I wrote as a graduate student in 1974 told me that my work was interesting and I should write it up for publication. And so I did.

This is the second edition of *Windows on the Workplace*, and its inception and research are very much inspired by younger workers who have updated the stories and helped me learn how it is for them in a workplace spread out over the globe, working in jobs far different from those detailed in the history of the last half of the twentieth century. Among the people who read and commented on this edition were Maria Carmen Dogerty, Maggie Dickinson, and Carol Oliver. As well, my appreciation goes to my very old friends Dean and Joan Heitner, John Welsh, Christine D'Ofrio and Marco Hernandez who always pay careful attention to detail and help to keep me on track to complete my work. And special thanks to Martin Paddio, Andrew Nash and Renee Pendergrass for shepherding me through the editorial process.

In particular I want to thank my children, all of whom are remarkably employed in freelance or serial positions that I could not have imagined twenty years ago. Brian, the oldest, is the only one in something closely related to an office job, yet he is based in Moscow, a financial officer for a Russian electronics chain. BJ, my stepdaughter, lives in Seattle, and when not churning out grant proposals on her computer in her garage/office is frequently seen in a kayak from which she coordinates environmental programs. Jesse is in New York, traveling from film set to commercial set to music video venues as he lugs his video and computer equipment to tape, edit, and produce films. And Bart has landed in Los Angeles where, after running a bakery for a supermarket and running his own catering business, he has kept to his interest in food and is now cooking in a restaurant.

My sister, also in Los Angeles and part of their generation, is a freelance TV producer, hopping from show to show and studio to studio, with detailed spreadsheets of the inner workings of production budgets on her computer. Special thanks also to my extended family who are moving through their thirties in rapidly changing terrains: David McKay, an immigration paralegal now plowing through an online degree; Chris Baker, a supermarket bakery manager about to find something else to do since the company has automated and centralized the bakery; and Andrew Mandell, carpenter, builder, writer, and musician.

These are their jobs as I write this. By the time you read this, they, like you and me, may be doing different work, in different places. I salute them for inspiring me to learn about how the world of work is changing, and I hope that I have helped them a little in demystifying the changes up until now.

When I was writing the first edition of this book my youngest son read through an early draft and said, "Mom, your generation spent so much time complaining about your jobs, and now you're complaining about there not being any jobs like the ones you didn't like!" I would like to think that this work is not trying to romanticize the past and that you, the readers, will use it to do more than complain about current economic conditions.

1. Introduction: Through the Looking Glass

Why does everyone want their documents sent to them yesterday?
— Office worker, 2003

Office work has changed a great deal over the last fifty years, but the pace of change increased to a gallop by the 1990s. Like the Red Queen in Lewis Carroll's *Through the Looking Glass,* people seem to be running faster and faster to stay in the same place. The media portrays changes in the workplace, particularly in offices, as the progress of high tech, making it seem as if "advances in technology" are inevitably leading to more and better jobs. Yet things are not always what they seem.

Obviously, workers who have had computers and other office technology plunked down on their desks have reason to believe that "advances in technology" have changed their working lives. But new pieces of office equipment don't simply arrive in people's cubicles. What is commonly lumped together as technology—everything from voice mail through software programs to networks—is specifically designed to fit in with management policies to cut labor costs and speed up the processing of information. Managerial objectives, and the technology designed to support them, are propelled along by a number of developments that are frequently clustered around the theme of increased global competition. In the name of meeting competition and decreasing costs, companies have taken steps to "reengineer" workplaces so that fewer people can do more work for less money, and so that work can be shunted or outsourced to any part of the globe for lower wages.

The way that work gets divided up into parcels and outsourced to sub-contractors as well as subcontinents did not come about suddenly. Throughout this book, we will see how developments since the 1950s have led to the workplaces of today. The examples in this and other chapters describe the changes as seen through the eyes of the workers affected, but each of the stories told is also analyzed in terms of the overall changes in the U.S. labor market. In the following example, Doug, a senior systems administrator, works for a New York–based multimedia firm that maintains computer servers for other Internet-based companies.[1] Doug feels lucky to have survived the dot-com job losses of 2001, but his job has been outsourced to three different companies in as many years, each time costing him financial loss and change of health insurance as well as fear of possible relocation.

"It used to be much more lively around here," he said as he escorted me down a dimly lit corridor of gray fabric cubicle partitions trimmed with red, matching the exposed red metal lights and air ducts hanging from the ceiling. "In 2000 I worked for [a well-known Internet firm] and we had six floors in this building. Now all you can see of the remains are a few pieces of art and some designer chairs near the elevator. And each of the floors in the building has been divided up into different companies."

Once inside Doug's cubicle we talked about his work, in between interruptions that included a beeping Instant Message (IM), a cell phone call, a pager, and a neighboring cubicle mate standing on his desk to hang over the partition and ask Doug how to do something. As a systems administrator he, along with three other people, is responsible for seeing that the computers that provide e-mail, Internet support, and general management information systems are running around the clock.

"It's a quiet day," he explained, as he talked about what he expected would be only a forty-hour workweek despite the fact that he had worked until 1 am the night before. Sometimes under project deadlines he works a seventy-hour week, and once a month, more or less, he is on call over the weekend. He was planning on getting married in a few months and he was concerned, as he put it, that "work can invade your life."

Doug administers Windows and Unix software and writes program scripts to provide automated tasks like adding and deleting users on the system and creating shared file directories. His job responsibilities have narrowed each time his section of the IT (Information Technology) department was sold to another firm. "It's not what I was planning on for a career, but sometimes the work is exciting, and I can take time off to work on a master's as long as I stay on call on my cell phone and check my e-mail."

When I met with him his biggest worry was about the rumors of moving his IT technical support group out of New York City. "I can see how they don't want to pay New York real estate costs to keep the computers here," he explained "so it makes sense for them to move this work out of here. If IT support moves to the parent company headquarters in Illinois I might be offered a position there, but I don't want to move. The more likely scenario, of course, is that IT support will be outsourced out of the country."

The Age of Insecurity

The second half of the twentieth century was to be the age of white-collar work—of jobs that were dependable, well paid, clean, and in nice workplaces. But the age of large, centralized offices, with traditional, well-defined jobs, turned out to be shorter than the industrial era that preceded it. More and more office jobs are being spread out over time and space, as the work is done at all times of the night and day by part-time and temporary workers in countries around the globe.

To be sure, the term *white collar* was coined earlier in the twentieth century to denote the starched white collars of the men, and a smattering of women wearing white shirtwaist blouses, whose collars marked them as having higher status and cleaner jobs than those in the so-called blue-collar factories. Today, few workers in office buildings actually wear white collars, while those working from home or on the go, may not wear collars at all, as they struggle to catch up with e-mail and mobile phone messages from vacations, cars, airplanes, beaches, or wherever.[2] Similarly, the term *position*, which for most of the twentieth century earmarked a person as having a place or location in an organization, began to drop out of use by the late 1990s. More commonly now, people apply for jobs or contracts, which can be temporary or certainly less fixed than career-oriented positions and may be based on projects, funding, or definable amount of work to be done.

In the 1960s, the United States moved from being classified as an industrial economy, one where the majority of jobs are in factories, to becoming a postindustrial economy based on service and office work. Today over 76 percent of the workforce is in the service sector, with more than 67 million people, or about 49 percent, in office-related jobs, which include managerial, professional, technical, and administrative-support categories.[3] But while white-collar work makes up almost half of all employment, its growth has slowed down, and jobs in services and sales, with lower wages and more part-time slots, have picked up.[4]

For many people, the restructuring of office work means less stability and security. Government and business reports tell us that we can expect to switch jobs and careers at least five times in our working lives. But this is the longer-term economic view. In everyday life it means that people already employed need to keep an eye out for the next job, while those trying to win a toehold in the office world need to compete with a growing number of people, many of whom have a wide range of skills.

The way work has been restructured is cloaked in simple-sounding terms like *reengineering, downsizing,* and *outsourcing* making it sound as if whatever happens is necessary and even inevitable. But in fact, beneath the made-up words lie seismic, structural shifts in the way the U.S. economy works. Reengineered workplaces in the 1990s were reorganized so that fewer people could do more work, thus leading to downsized organizations where corporate executives got to buy, sell, and trade their companies for more because there were fewer workers and therefore the labor costs were lower. Outsourcing, or the sending of jobs outside of the company where they once were done—whether to another smaller firm within the same building, like Doug's, or across the world—also lowers labor costs as well as fixed costs of operation, such as building leases and heat and electricity. Like downsizing, outsourcing lets corporations show fewer expenses on the balance sheets, which in theory makes the organization more attractive to investors as well as mergers and acquisitions with other firms. This process takes different forms in different organizations, but the effect on the workers is often quite similar, as we will see in the following examples.

George is the deputy city editor of a large metropolitan newspaper. When I met him in 1992, the newspaper had been bought out by a huge multinational media firm that had made its mark around the world by standardizing newspapers. The new owner made it clear not only that he wanted to break the newspaper unions, but that he was intent on streamlining the newspaper process, producing short, tabloid stories that were of high reader interest but were low on traditional costly research techniques.

When George greets me the offices are almost soundless. George usually makes himself walk over and talk to the reporters when he assigns stories, but this is not generally done: most people send each other e-mail messages with completed stories or works-in-progress as attachments.

George has been in the newspaper business for more than twenty years. "I could spend a whole day now without any voice conversation with reporters. I could do my job sitting at home with an Internet connection, a fax, and computer. I can't explain what a story needs via e-mail as well as I can in person, but that's the way it's done today." Story conferences, the meetings in which editors and reporters discuss news items and plan how to cover them, have been eliminated.

Gone as well is the telephone switchboard, where cub reporters got practice answering phones and passing on important messages. "I hate this voice-mail system," George says, "because you need a human to interpret a message. Like how the hell are you supposed to go after hot tips if the caller can only leave a message on your machine? Management is thrilled," he adds, "because they can continue to cut staff."

It's particularly irritating to the reporters that the voice-messaging system "automatically" puts incoming calls into voice mail when the reporters are on another call. George explains: "This is a business where you have to have a line open for someone to call you back. But the minute you pick up the phone to make a call, the next call goes into the so-called voice-message place." He compares this voice-mail problem to the "pain of a computer system" that was set up to eliminate typographers and in the process messed up editing by changing the rewriting process. "It's another case of engineering winning out over the editorial process," he says.

Proponents of high tech tell us that offices like George's are the "the way things are." Back in 1992 the fact that George didn't have to see people to get his job done meant that his job, like many others, was being set up to join what is called the "virtual office." His work, like the work of the reporters, can be done anywhere and at any time of day, in effect speeding up reporting time and cutting down on office space. Still, for George all this speeding up and cutting out means editors and reporters have less time to research stories and less of a say in finishing them off. In effect he is now part of a process that produces a standardized, tabloid-style product that differs markedly from the newspaper before the takeover, but looks a lot like other newspapers around the world. Today we see these changes not only in newspapers, but also in the format of television and Internet news where small units of "information" are almost instantaneously dispensed from mobile reporters with mobile equipment. Research and fact-checking take a backseat to getting the information out fast.

Specialists in office IT, like systems analysts, consultants, and researchers, argue that systems that don't support the way the work is done are examples of poor system design. Certainly the limited voice-mail operation and the design of a one-size-fits-all computer system that ignores the editorial process are examples of this. Yet this type of "poor" technical design is often chosen over other ways of designing systems not out of stupidity or bad management—as systems analysts tend to think—but because it meets cost-cutting objectives and, most important, also controls the workers caught up in its web.

Changes in work and office technology take many shapes, often beginning with the redesign of a job so that pieces of it can be done faster and more cheaply. George's work is an example of a professional job that senior-level managers classify as being difficult to cut into pieces, although we will see that this has been done throughout the publishing industry. Sheila's work, described in the next story is, on the other hand, more typical of the type of "back-office" job in a law firm, that has over the last dozen years or so has become both more routinized and less in demand.

Sheila started as a Wang operator (an early word-processing system) in 1980. When I initially interviewed her in late 1993, the law firm she then worked for, which had over one hundred attorneys, was about to merge with a larger firm. As part of the merger plan, arrangements were being made to phase out the old Wang system and transfer everything over to a networked PC-based word-processing system. This is what I saw in the word-processing center where Sheila worked:

> Sheila sat in her own enclosed office and supervised an operation that ran twenty-four hours a day, seven days a week, and was staffed by fifteen operators, all of whom were temporary workers. "More attorneys are doing their own word processing now, but the complicated documents and the long ones still come down here," she said. The operators had to be highly skilled. In 1993 they were using two different systems (Wang and PC).

> Sheila's operation included document scanners and fax machines. Behind her office was a large temperature-controlled equipment room for the huge Wang storage files and the computer system. After the merger her work involved much more technical trouble-shooting than it used to. As part of the merger plan, the word-processing center was being restructured as a document-processing center, requiring new and more complicated software to fit in with the different work practices of the two firms.

By 1995, Sheila was no longer employed at the law firm. As a result of the merger, she was replaced by the supervisor from the other firm. Although Sheila had a wide range of technical skills, she was viewed as the "Wang expert," and the old Wangs were being replaced by PCs. Other changes took place as well, affecting everyone in the law firm. Upstairs in the front offices where the attorneys sat, computers were on every desk. All the lawyers had been trained in Windows-based word-processing software (WordPerfect at that time) and were expected to do almost all of their own document processing. Secretaries had been "tripled up," and those who remained handled billing, time sheets, and some letters. The document-processing center was still used for spillover work, but most of it was being done at night and on weekends. All of the workers were part-time word processors supplied by temporary agencies. Word processing, which was a new and rapidly growing job area in the early 1980s, was by the mid-1990s beginning to decline not only in law firms but in most organizations.

By 2003, the law firm had again merged and most of the overnight document center, along with massive scanning and indexing operations, was outsourced to Asia. Changes for attorneys were also extensive, as almost all now did their own documents, relying on not just word-processing software as they did in the 1990s, but software that can access templates for legal forms and databases. As one lawyer explained it, "We are almost always assembling pieces of forms and documents that we e-mail to each other—practically never having to draft from scratch." Following another merger, almost a third of the attorneys were laid off.

After some time, Sheila got a job as a night-shift supervisor in another law firm, making less than she did before. Roger, on the other hand, as a temporary worker for an insurance company, started with fewer skills and less security than Sheila. Like the changes in Sheila's law firm, much of the downsizing and reorganization in the insurance industry intensified in the 1990s. While Roger could get by on his salary as a temp, the insurance company he worked for found it could get by without him. The firm, like others in the insurance field, ordered a new computer system that was designed to replace the back-office clerical work of assembling insurance policies. Here is how it happened from Roger's perspective:

> "For me, [the computer system's arrival] in St. Paul was heralded with a job fair in early 1991. It was a casting call for people with clerical skills and career motivation. Nearly five hundred applicants showed up for full-time policy assembly, data-entry, and clerical jobs." But, Roger continues, "by the following summer, what had been called 'career opportunities' were disappearing. In one division, eighteen full-time assemblers had been cut to six. The rest of us were temps. It was not a happy place."[5]

> Roger was employed during the time when the new system was being phased in and more than a hundred people, taking up a whole floor of an office building, were let go, signaling to him that "the job of policy assembly went the way of the buggy whip." Outside of enjoying the daily banter with his coworkers, this was never what he would call a "great job." Yet the demise of entry-level jobs like this has implications for other workers on the bottom rungs of office work. Roger explained it this way:

Workers taking telephone and online orders. (AP Photo/Peter Cosgrove)

"Policy assembly is the traditional entry-level job in service-center work. Some underwriters began here. With this job vanishing, the entry-level stakes move higher: when the data-entry job vanishes with the advent of the 'paperless office,' the first rung on the employment ladder will be out of reach for many traditional beginning workers. And the heap of dislocated workers will become bigger."

From the insurance company's perspective, the new computer system was a rational step in integrating the handling of policies, cutting down paperwork, and speeding up processing. Indeed, when it was designing and installing the system, the company broke all work tasks down into what they called "work units" and estimated that by the end of the phase-in period, the decrease in the number of work units would have cut costs in half. Office automation in the insurance field has been around since the early days of large mainframe computers in the late 1950s, but, as discussed in the coming chapters, it took the better part of the last thirty years for companies like those in insurance to learn enough about the workflow to be able to cut it up into individual steps and then integrate the steps into software programs.

Meanwhile, the automation of clerical work in front offices has followed a different pattern, but the result, when combined with management reorganization and job redesign, has also been heightened insecurity for the individuals affected. Secretarial jobs, for example, have been declining as former clerical functions are pushed onto the desks of managers and professionals, as shown in the example of the law firm. In some cases former secretaries have been able to grab some of the newer positions as administrative and executive assistants. But even from this vantage point there are problems. Here is how it looked for Glenda, who worked as an executive assistant in an office of a large telecommunications company providing land-line phone service in the mid-1990s:

> She sits in a tiny half-glass partitioned cubicle. "I don't type, file, or answer the phone," she says proudly. "I love voice mail because it freed me from having to be chained to my desk." The company used to have a hierarchical structure where people were promoted from step to step, but the job titles have been collapsed into only a few levels after reorganization in the early 1990s. The next rung above her, the "members of technical staff" (who make up most of the office), do all their own word processing, answer their own phones, and use voice mail and e-mail for their messages.
>
> Glenda describes her job as that of "a buffer, someone who helps things run smoothly." She had worked as an executive secretary for a computer company, but she likes this job much better. "If people need conference rooms, moving requests, or travel reservations, they e-mail me and I get it done for them." Although she likes it when people come by and "make personal contact," she would rather they send requests by e-mail so that she can have a written record of what they want.

Glenda loved her work and the fact that e-mail and voice mail freed her from the telephone, but the large company she worked for didn't have many administrative assistants, which meant that her workload was increasing. In the '90s almost all support services below Glenda's level—from the copy shop to the mailroom—were performed by temporary workers. Now, however, after two further telecom mergers, those positions are mostly outsourced. Indeed, the company drastically cut its full-time permanent staff after it merged with a larger regional phone company and has since sharply cut employment following its acquisition by a telecommunications giant.[6]

This telecommunications company, like Roger's insurance firm, Sheila's law firm, George's newspaper, and Doug's Internet company, follow a pattern where fewer people are doing more work, usually because several tasks, and sometimes several jobs, have been combined into one. The use of voice mail, e-mail, the Internet, and computer information systems enable organizations to *further* combine and integrate jobs. But in all cases it was not just the technology that made it happen, but management-sponsored work reorganization, including collapsed job ladders and job redesign, resulting in "everything rolled-into-one" jobs. Often the management-induced changes in work organization appear faddish and wrongheaded like those of the bumbling bosses in the 1999 film *Office Space* or the cartoon "Dilbert." Yet the pattern of work reorganization, as seen over several decades, is more consistent. And as organizations cut costs by cutting people they try to enhance their standing in financial markets, making it possible to merge and acquire other firms. Clearly this last step can be beneficial to stockholders, but it increases feelings of insecurity as office workers caught in the crossfire of merged companies fear (with real reason) their jobs will be cut or they will be moved to other locations, uprooting themselves and their families.

The Freelancing of America

The old contract between employer and employee, which came into being at the start of the industrial period in the late eighteenth century, moved the workplace out of the home, collecting workers under one roof—the factory—and setting a fixed time period for labor. This contract, or set of expectations, was carried over into the early postindustrial period and shaped office work as it developed in the mid-twentieth century. But now, as the traditional bonds between employer and employee are being cut, increasing numbers of workers look at job markets where they may not expect, and indeed may not want to work, for a single employer.

Economists refer to this recent change in employment relations as part of a process that is good for increasing profits and accumulating capital.

Some call it "flexible accumulation." The flexibility comes from passing the risks that organizations and managers used to "own" on to individual workers. And this flexibility of labor has become a cornerstone of what the business press calls the "New Economy." As we saw in the last section, for individuals caught in the switch from more permanent employer-employee relations to freelance or contractual work, heightened insecurity—financial, social, and emotion—may be the marker of how these workers experience the change. But for other, usually younger workers, the expectation of a full-time, more permanent contract with a single employer may no longer be the norm for office and professional work. For all, however, sharing the risks of employment means having to think and plan about where the next paycheck will come from and, significantly for those in the United States, having to worry about health insurance.

In 1995 the U. S. Department of Labor and its adjunct the Bureau of Labor Statistics (BLS) began counting contingent workers. Their definition of contingent workers as "persons who do not expect their jobs to last or who report that their jobs are temporary" has been expanded to include people in what they call "alternative work arrangements" such as independent contractors, on-call workers (those called in only as needed), people employed by temporary help agencies, and those who are hired by contract or subcontract firms. Statistics for contingent and nontraditional job categories are not collected regularly, but BLS estimates in 2001 showed that in addition to the almost 5.5 million people who listed themselves as contingent workers, there were also 8.6 million independent contractors, 2.1 million workers called in as needed, 1.2 million workers with temporary help agencies, and more than 600,000 working for contractors. This means that over 18 million people in the BLS sample had no ongoing contract with their employer and, for the most part, no benefits. It is unclear what percentage of these workers are in professional, technical, or administrative white-collar work, but the growth of independent contractors, the largest category, is fueled by managerial and professional people setting up their own businesses.[7]

While office workers have experienced the ups and downs of business cycles throughout the twentieth century, it was not until the corporate reengineering of the early '90s that contractual or more permanent employment began to erode in most job categories. This relatively quick shift to a post-employment contract system of flexible labor relations came about at a period in time when companies had reengineered jobs, merged with other firms, outsourced work, and introduced successive waves of new computer-based systems. It is no surprise that many people believe it was technology that brought about change in their employment status since technology is more visible than the behind-the-scene management deci-sion-making that leads to creating an economic environment for flexible accumulation.

A common characteristic of most self-employed people doing freelance work is that the work has been carved out of pieces that used to be done by full-time workers working on payroll within the walls of an organization. Like part-time work and outsourced jobs, freelance arrangements tear the bind between employer and employee. In many instances the change is about when people are paid for the work they do. Under the old industrial and office pattern, people were paid for the hours they worked, making pay linked to *time*. Now, however, for much freelance work pay is linked not so much to time, but rather to projects, or pieces of work—in other words, pay is linked to a finished or defined product or service. This has the effect, as we will see, of making workers double and triple up on the number of things they do in any one period of time, in order to hedge their risk, and make enough to cover monthly expenses.

Some industries have been outsourcing work to freelancers for a rela-tively long period of time. Publishing, for example, has worked out a con-tract system for writing, editing, and copyediting books since the 1960s, particularly for school textbooks. Emily has worked at home since 1969 when, for a combination of reasons, she left a large publishing house and started editing and writing at home.

> *Emily's home office is well established, since it's been her work site for more than three decades. She has created a work space made up of an old library table, a bookcase, a computer desk, and an assortment of shelves and hanging file folders over the desk space. Unlike some people who carve their home offices out of closet or basement space, Emily has her*

office set up in a sunny corner room in her house. "I spend so much time here," she explains, "that it's got to be a place I want to be in."

"I like working at home," she says, "because it gives me the chance to make my own schedule, although sometimes that's really a mixed blessing, particularly when a number of deadlines come crashing down around holidays. Had I gone back to the publishing house I used to work for, I doubt that I would have gotten to do such a wide range of things from researching, writing, and now authoring books."

But for Emily and her colleagues the pace and intensity of work has been speeding up. "Deadlines are coming faster, as the shelf-life of school textbooks has gone down from five years to two or three years. Also," she adds, "publishers want more and more material packaged with each book, including bloated teacher's editions with more step-by-step exercises."

Emily, with her experience and contacts, now works for royalty fees that increase her income over the more traditional arrangement of "work-for-hire," where writers are paid by the page or chapter. Work-for-hire in the textbook field is generally arranged through detailed specifications that call for such specifics as the number of words on a page, the format of the examples and exercises, and a detailed breakdown of subject headings.

This piecemeal approach to writing textbooks is not unlike arrangements in other areas like engineering or computer programming where the contractual specifications detail the pieces of work to be done, making it easier for subcontracting firms to hire individuals to complete separate, and more controllable, parts of a project; parts of work which in turn can be contracted out to individuals or consulting groups anywhere in the world.

Yet the blending of work space and home space implied by the flexibility of work that can be done anywhere brings new sets of problems, as illustrated by the following account, adapted from a New York Times article[8]:

Peggy spends a lot of time on the phone in her car. As an advertising executive, she is one of about forty employees in her company who have been shifted to the "virtual office." The new corporate headquarters is being renovated into "non-territorial offices," places where an ad executive can check in and be temporarily assigned a workspace. Peggy jokes that "we are going from cubes to cubbies," because the space in the new office will be more like a library carrel or a booth in an airport executive lounge than an office cubicle.

Peggy, with Powerbook, modem, portable phone, and e-mail, is a telecommuter. Whether in her home, the front seat of her car, an airport terminal, or a client's office, she can send in her work, check for messages, and look at client data on her computer. Many management proponents of telecommuting and virtual offices claim that professional workers gain a lot from the arrangement. Peggy is not so sure: it seems to her that her work is expanding to fill all her working hours. Picking up her daughter from nursery school, running household errands, and finding a quiet place to do creative work all vie for her time. As she puts it, "I have the feeling that it is no longer my life fitting into my work, but my work fitting into my life."

Peggy's plight, while sounding contemporary, described her situation a decade ago, before the widespread use of the Internet, mobile phones, and lap and palm devices. It was also before so many professional jobs were moved out of organizations into cars, homes, and "virtual spaces." The pattern and pace of Peggy's work has today become far more common for far more people than it was in the '90s.

Things Are Not Always What They Seem

Magazines and radio and TV talk shows make it sound as if the "advent," or sudden appearance of new technology, is the driving force in changing work. And the popular press makes it seem like high-tech jobs are cutting a path to a high-skill, high-wage future. But there is little evidence to support this. Like Alice in the strange landscape of the Looking Glass, we find ourselves in need of a map to show us where we have been and help us figure out where we want to go. When you read magazines or listen to talk shows, you might think that it is technology alone that has the majority of office workers spending their days peering at computer screens in their multiple roles as finders, assemblers, and keepers of information.

But the idea that technology *advances* work makes technology sound like the chess pieces that move themselves in *Alice in Wonderland*. To understand what is happening today, we need to move beyond make-believe and take a clear look around. Whatever technological "advancement" is, it is a rocky road when seen through the eyes of the workers and managers caught in the process.

Unfortunately, the glowing language of advancement has kept us from looking closely at the changes that are taking place in the workplace, and at how technology has been designed to support these changes. As the upcoming chapters in this book will show, technologies, like personal computers, laptops, and the Internet, were not just invented and introduced into organizations. Rather, developments in different technologies have been tried out over many decades, often long before they got sold and used.

If you look around, you can easily find many people you know who have stories to tell about how their work has changed or is changing. Some of the things people talk about concern new computer systems, but many others focus on work reorganization, company policies, and issues of job security. Until the early 1990s, most office workers had fairly well-defined occupational titles and worked in more-or-less traditional office settings. Today, people who enter the labor market, as well as those already in it, are finding themselves with brand-new job titles, as well as in jobs without a title, and in a wide variety of workplaces, not just office cubicles.

Two economic issues have become strikingly clear. The first deals with the restructuring of the *labor market,* where people compete for jobs and hope they have the right skills and experience. As corporate and in-house organizational jobs are dismantled, more people are being pushed into highly competitive *labor markets* for short-term, temporary, or freelance jobs. This has the effect of keeping salaries and wages down as more people compete for a smaller number of relatively secure jobs. A second issue concerns the restructuring of the *labor process,* or the way the work is done. More jobs and pieces of jobs have been combined, making work more intensive. And as virtually all office workers need to use computers to get their jobs done, more are expected to have computer skills—so that managers don't necessarily have to pay them for these skills.

Labor market and labor process changes are happening all over the world as the process of globalization gallops around the globe. Globalization takes on more complex patterns when we study it up close,

Telephone workers in Brazil, 1998. (AP Photo/Dario Lopez-Mills)

because it requires companies to constantly search for cheaper markets to supply the labor (people) to provide goods and services. Markets, in turn, take on deeper meanings when we examine how nation-states and regions compete to provide either the cheapest labor and/or the biggest consumer spending areas. Globalization is not new, nor is the creation of new world-wide markets. Capitalism as an economic system is based on organizations expanding to gain more capital to finance still more profit-making ventures. This process of capitalist expansion, currently tagged as globalization, is a process that requires corporations to try to expand beyond any border and to seek out increasingly flexible ways (generally meaning those areas with fewer regulations) of accumulating capital. What is new now is that the speed with which corporations can move both capital and labor around the world has markedly increased.

Certainly the introduction of Information Technology has had an important role in speeding up this global and flexible expansion process. IT is also a factor in bringing about changes in both the conditions of global labor markets and the intensity of the way work gets done (labor process) in countries around the world. There is no question that the falling prices of all kinds of office technology, including copiers, computers, fax machines, voice mail, telephone systems, and mobile technologies, coupled with standardization and the availability of less expensive software, has made it easier for management to justify introducing new office systems and shifting work around among countries. But stories of workplace change need to be told in context, and the context includes not just the technology but also the reasons for its use. The restructuring of work that has occurred did not come about overnight; nor did it come about by whim or accident.

This book tells the story of changes in office work from the 1950s through today in the United States, the way work has been organized in each period, and the ways that technology has been shaped in order to support particular forms of work organization. None of the developments, in and of themselves, are inevitable. Further, what is good for an individual company is not necessarily good for the workers in that company or for the larger economy and society.

The next chapter looks at developments in office work in the 1950s and 1960s, highlighting the rise of multinational corporations and how corporate values such as rigid hierarchy and paternalistic management shaped office work then. It uses two seemingly different occupations, secretaries and computer programmers, to illustrate how work was divided and office automation was first applied to the back office.

Chapter 3 looks at office work and technology in the 1970s. During that period, most companies tried to pattern work after factory systems, pushing for jobs with an increased number of routine and repetitive functions. Computer programs were designed and programmed as "data processing" systems to fit this pattern.

Chapter 4 focuses on the 1980s, a period of flux and contradiction for the organization of office work and the technology used to support it. The decade opened with much talk of the "office of the future" and the "paperless office," but it wasn't until mid-decade that personal computers and fax machines became common, and it wasn't until the end of the decade that voice mail and telecom networks made it possible to scatter office work—leading up to the so-called virtual office of the late 1990s. Management theory and practice were almost equally divided during this period between continuing the routinization of work so common in the 1960s and 1970s and integrating and combining functions into new job categories.

Sometimes management plans for greater efficiency and office automation didn't fit together. In the 1950s and 1960s, for example, making office work fit a factory assembly-line model sometimes made it take longer to get some things done and resulted in clumsy computer systems. In the 1980s, office systems were supposed to bring about a paperless office, but by all accounts more and more paperwork was created.[9] The rocky road of technical change is littered with proposals that highlight contradictions and clashes between management plans and workplace practice.

The 1990s, the subject of chapters 5 and 6, are like a braid weaving together the developments that began in the earlier periods. Work that had already been routinized could now be outsourced. And newly integrated forms of work led to fewer people working longer hours or more intensely, doing work that had previously been done by more people. Chapter 6 views the strands of the braid that weave a social and political history of the Internet, together with management plans for reorganizing office work. Most Internet history focuses on the names and dates of the men who invented the thing we call the Internet, but the history narrated here emphasizes how Internet software and hardware were redesigned and used to support the economic and political realities of the late twentieth century.

The rapidly changing picture of current forms of work is the subject of chapter 7. From all accounts it has become clear that the "office of the future" is everywhere. Here the ways that workers experience the shifting sands of time and place, home and work, and the permeable and overlapping borders between their public and their private lives, are explored. Examples in this chapter focus on two distinctly different types of knowledge work, college teaching and software development. But people in both settings have witnessed work that has been cut into piecework and made into part-time and outsourced jobs, many of which are no longer done in the "knowledge economy" of the United States.

Chapter 8 closes with an analysis of all these developments and looks at change as a process—a process that can be influenced. In particular it looks back at issues like skill and analyzes how and why skills get reshuffled into different jobs, done in different countries, as well as how skills get embedded into software programs. Routinized work, often called "deskilled" work, and integrated work, referred to as "upskilled" or "reskilled" work, are two pieces of the same pattern: according to management theory, tasks can be integrated only after routine functions have been identified and sorted out. And software can only be written and sold as programs after routine functions and tasks have been clearly identified so that they can be coded into programs.

Office and information technology grows out of software—the instructions that drive the programs as well as the databases that provide the data, or raw fuel, of information technology. In chronicling the creation of the so-called knowledge or information society this book documents the ways in which human skill and knowledge have been abstracted from worker control and coded into software or entered into databases. Some of the ways that this process has occurred have been designed and planned, while others happened as the software and data got used by more people and were changed with use, which the brief history of the Internet has demonstrated.

Office technology—computers, laptops, copiers, fax machines, mobile phones, handheld devices, voice mail, and the like—is fundamentally a social development because hardware and software are created by people, and they are used, changed, and reused by people. If this book were a murder mystery, we would discover that it wasn't technology that "did it," but the people who make the decisions about what technology is designed for and how it is used. The next chapter sets the stage for this story.

2. The 1950s and 1960s:
Dawn of the Computer Age

In the enormous file of the office, in all the calculating rooms, accountants and purchasing agents replace the man who did his own figuring. And in the lower reaches of the white-collar world, office operatives grind along, loading and emptying the filing system; there are private secretaries and typists, entry clerks, billing clerks, corresponding clerks—a thousand kinds of clerks; the operators of light machinery, comptometers, dictaphones, addressographs; and the receptionists to let you in or keep you out.

—C. Wright Mills, *White Collar,* 1951

Most of the lower-income white-collar jobs that sociologist C. Wright Mills described in his classic book *White Collar* are gone now, or are performed in totally different ways.[1] Yet his description of the "enormous file of the office" sets the stage for understanding the beginning of what came to be known among social scientists and the media as the Computer and Information Age. This period, which began after the Second World War, has also been given a string of titles that refer to its apparently "revolutionary" nature, hinting that the computer, information, and organizational revolutions would bring us into a new era of easier living and better jobs.

This optimism rested on two pillars of change after the Second World War: the global expansion of businesses, which created the need for more information in the form of documents to record transactions, and the growing reliance on office technology to support these new functions. The first resulted in an increase in the number of office workers needed to operate the new machines and handle all the documents. The second, the growing reliance on office technology, initially supported the clerical and operator jobs that Mills described but later led to enormous changes in their numbers and function.

What's Good for the Country?

> What is good for General Motors is good for the country.
> —Charles Wilson, Secretary of Defense under Dwight D. Eisenhower

As a child growing up in the 1950s, I learned that the United States was the "best of all possible places." We were taught to expect continued economic growth, more and more jobs, growing prosperity, and a better standard of living, all of which were to be brought to us by companies like General Electric, which, to paraphrase its advertising slogan, "brings good things to life." But the world was not always like a scene from the TV sitcom *Father Knows Best*. I remember asking a lot of questions during the recession of 1957–58, when the news shows were telling us that the recession was caused by "people not buying enough." If we would only go out and buy more cars and home appliances, the economy would get back on track—or so we were told. But it didn't make sense to me that it was the consumers' fault that the economy wasn't growing. Nor did it make sense that the General Motors plant down the road from my father's hardware store had laid off thousands of workers who certainly couldn't be better consumers if they weren't getting paid. To my young eyes, what was merely a problem for General Motors, or General Electric, or any of the other big companies, was a disaster for the people who worked for them. And so in the 1960s I went to college to study economics, only to find that mainstream economists propagated this same belief in the ability of companies to create job growth and a higher a standard of living for all.

It is true that in the 1950s and 1960s, the number of steady jobs was increasing, productivity was up, and the economy, despite a few recessions

A secretarial pool, late 1940s. [Culver Pictures]

along the way, was growing. But this growth was not the result of individual companies "doing the right thing"; rather, it was based primarily on the economic and military dominance that the United States had won for itself following the destruction of the other big economies in the Second World War. U.S. companies were in a sense the "only game in town," the only companies able to meet the growing worldwide demand for goods and services.

The language and ideology of global competition and increased productivity that we hear today is almost a rerun (with some new words thrown in) of what I heard in the 1950s. We are still told that our job as consumers is to keep the economy strong, and that we need to increase our productivity so that we can help U.S. companies compete in the heated-up global marketplace. Since factory work has already been pressed into more flexible production through the use of automation and assembly lines, the emphasis has shifted to making middle-class white-collar workers, who came into prominence in the 1950s, just as flexible.[2]

White-Collar Workers Arrive

According to C. Wright Mills, "In the early nineteenth century, although there are no exact figures, probably four-fifths of the occupied population were self-employed enterprisers. By 1870, only about one-third, and by 1940, only about one-fifth, were still in the 'old' middle class."[3] These small entrepreneurs—shop owners, small-business owners, merchants, traders, and farmers—had accumulated enough money to own independent property and thus earn their own living. But by the end of the nineteenth century, many businesses were big enough and strong enough to begin to buy out smaller and weaker companies, beginning the march toward monopolies and large industrial holdings. By the 1950s, the United States had been transformed from a nation of small farmers and entrepreneurs into a nation of employees. One group of these new employees was made up of white-collar workers, who were becoming the backbone of a "new" middle class.

In the years after the Second World War, white-collar work was seen as a ticket to upward mobility. Housing prices were comparatively low and a great deal of affordable housing was being built for returning soldiers. Support for the housing boom came, in part, from the government's policy of ensuring low-cost mortgages to potential home buyers. At the same time, low-cost loans for GIs to go to college meant that there were a growing number of better-educated men (and comparatively few women) who formed a ready pool of white-collar labor. The new middle class owned property, but not the kind or amount that would make them into entrepreneurs or people owning their own businesses. Thus the American Dream shifted. Owning homes and cars replaced owning shops, businesses, and the means of production (property and tools controlled by an owner). In essence, the entrepreneurial culture of the nineteenth century was replaced by a new corporate one.

The growing prominence of corporations was one cornerstone of this period. Working as a salaried white-collar employee for "the organization" provided solid benefits, prestige, security, and the opportunity for promotion. Corporate life, while bureaucratic and regimented, provided a career, not just a job. That is, it did this for those who fit the model of the newly emerging corporate world—people who, prior to the civil rights movement of the 1950s and 1960s and the women's movement of the 1970s and 1980s, were primarily white, college-educated men. Indeed, government policy and social pressure following the Second World War were set up to push women out of the labor force.[4] But in the 1950s, 1960s, and early 1970s, the demand for white-collar workers was generally greater than the supply of people coming into the labor market. So a small but significant number of educated and trained women were accepted into clerical, administrative, and some professional positions in this period.

Corporate and business expansion was fueled by the growth of huge government-sponsored programs to mass-produce weapons and supplies for the military. It was also sparked by large organizations taking advantage of U.S. military supremacy in much of the non-Communist world by expanding their businesses into third world countries, where they were able to win access to cheap resources and cheaper labor. Defense Secretary Charles Wilson was half right—U.S. military and political power was good for General Motors, and for General Electric, General Mills, and the generals, both private and public, who profited from international expansion.

The new multinational trade expansion was founded on corporate rules and practices that were based on standardization, routinization, and belief in the efficiency of bureaucratic policy. Bureaucracy was not new. It had been seen in military form in the nineteenth century and was analyzed and critiqued by the German sociologist Max Weber back at the turn of the twentieth century. Centralization of administration and control of operations was a first principle of bureaucracy. This type of centralized administration was backed by hierarchical rules and carried out using an intensive division of labor and standardization of tasks. Large national and multinational corporations applied these ideas to white-collar work, showing that office tasks could be divided and thus, like factory tasks, become more easily controlled. In the 1950s, bureaucratic principles and practices were applied on an international scale.

For the most part, the popular press portrayed bureaucratic corporate life as part and parcel of "getting a good job." Yet the dark side of life in an organization was visible as well. Novels like *The Man in the Gray Flannel Suit* and studies like William Whyte's *The Organization Man* addressed the

The Rise and Fall of Secretarial Work

1873   When the YWCA trains eight women to work on typewriters, doctors are asked to certify that the women are physically and mentally strong enough to do the job.

1875   A want ad for female typists appears in a New York newspaper. It reads: "Mere girls are now earning from $10 to $20 a week with the 'Type-Writer.'"

1900   According to the Census Bureau, there are more than 100,000 people working as secretaries, stenographers, and typists.

1911   The Katharine Gibbs secretarial school is founded. It not only teaches typewriting and office skills, but also specializes in teaching proper behavior and dress. White gloves are its graduates' trademarks.

1920   There are more than 1 million women clerical workers.

1960   Of the more than 1.4 million secretaries in the United States, only 42,000 (or 2.9 percent) are men.

1990s   The number of secretaries in the United States reached 3.397 million in 1994, before layoffs began to seriously effect this occupational category.

2002   Secretarial positions as an occupational category lose 1 million members, down to 2.3 million.

2003   Bureau of Labor Statistics lumps secretaries together with administrative assistants, with the latter as the growing occupational group.

Sources include: U.S. Congress, Office of Technology Assessment, *Automating America's Offices* (Washington, D.D.: 1985); Lupton, *Mechanical Brides*; and Marjorie Wolfe, "But How Fast Can You Type, Sir," *New York Times,* May 22, 1994, p. B10; Bureau of Labor Statistics, Employment and Earnings, Household Data Annual Averages Table II, 1990–2003.

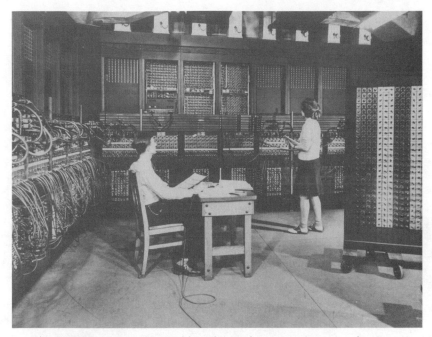

The ENIAC computer, 1946. Although it took up an entire room, the ENIAC was far slower and had a fraction of the storage capacity of today's desktop PC. [IBM Archives]

problems of conformity and stress. The "organization man" (and he was a man) came to typify the period of corporate expansion. As we will see in the following examples, this period was one where the foundations of divided and controlled work were established inside office walls. At the same time that front-office, sometimes prestigious, jobs were made to appear to be personifications of corporate life, many tasks were being divided and separated into lower-paid back-office functions. The divide-and-conquer approach made few distinctions between the established area of clerical work and the newly minted field of computer programming.

Dividing Front from Back Offices

By the 1950s secretarial and clerical work was a well-accepted field for women. But it wasn't always that way. Before the 1880s, clerical work was done by men, who were viewed by owners and managers as possible recruits into the business.

Oddly enough, the "feminization" of clerical work had something to do with the introduction of machinery, in this case typewriters. In 1874 Remington, a manufacturer of guns, began to mass-produce "type writers." Since typewriting as a job was too new to have any particular association with men or women, the use of female "type-writers"—as the occupation was first called—was not perceived as a threat to male secretaries. In this way, the use of the keyboard, and indeed the use of office equipment in general, became associated with women's work.

But it was also the growth of the field that gave women a chance to "step up" to office work. At the turn of the century, as business and the associated paperwork expanded, there was a growing demand for clerical workers, and at the same time there were more educated women who needed to work. These two trends together created an opening for women who previously had only the choice of factory work or servant positions.[5] After the Second World War, and especially in the 1950s, when women working in male-defined positions were stigmatized socially, they were allowed to stay in the comparatively lower-paid secretarial and clerical areas. This was in part because their use of typewriters, stenographic equipment, and adding machines was already accepted. Such work provided opportunities for women from a range of ethnic and racial backgrounds, as well as acceptable openings for both older and married women. Meanwhile, the positions that some women had formerly held, such as supervisory jobs, were becoming part of a new corporate executive career track—the mid-twentieth-century way to recruit men into the business world.

Despite its low pay, office work was viewed as relatively safe, clean, and of higher status than factory or domestic work. More than a hundred years ago, in 1890, female typists earned 1.8 times more than women factory workers, but by the 1950s routine clerical jobs paid less than factory jobs: the status and security of the work were more attractive than the pay.[6]

The word *secretary* originally came from the word secret, which implies a role for somone, "entrusted with secrets." In other words, a secretary was someone who could act as a gatekeeper, guarding the secrets of the boss and carrying out a wide range of decisions and tasks that were often invisible to him.[7] Clerical work, an even broader category, began to be carved out of secretarial functions in the early part of the twentieth century, and by the 1950s it included typists, file clerks, and large numbers of people doing the behind-the-scenes work of keeping documents and papers in order—carrying out what managers saw as the housework of the office.

The visible parts of secretarial work, like typing and filing, have increasingly been separated, reutilized, and automated, while the more invisible tasks, such as gatekeeping, as well as prioritizing the boss's work, scheduling, and making the office run smoothly, have resisted—at least until recently—such routinization and automation. Managers and efficiency experts (the forerunners of today's management consultants) made the visible tasks into back-office functions, while the harder to quantify and therefore more difficult to routinize secretarial work stayed in the front office.

In the 1950s, this splitting of back- from front-office functions was also a dividing line between mechanized functions and those that used very little in the way of equipment. Until the widespread use of the word processor, for example, secretaries used typewriters, dictaphones, and telephones, while the machines for calculating, copying, addressing, and performing other specialized functions were put where those entering the office would not see them.

This type of division of routine from non-routine tasks followed management objectives for increasing productivity and control over the growing clerical workforce. The routine work being done in the back office took many forms: there were bank check processors working with MICR (magnetic ink character recognition) machines, keypunch operators and verifiers, duplicating machine operators, mainframe computer operators in glassed-in "operations rooms," and, of course, typists. The split in pay scales and working environments was a concrete reminder of the physical separation of front- and back-office functions.

In the 1960s, upper management pushed for, and got, separate typing pools—areas usually in the basement or some other out-of-the-way place where work could be "sent down" to typists whose sole function was to type and send the finished product "back up." Many managers at first did not like this breakdown of what Barbara Garson, in her book *The*

Electronic Sweatshop, called "office monogamy"—the one boss–one secretary relationship—but management experts argued that it was much more efficient.[8] Typing pools, which were much later to become word-processing centers, were the result of a division of labor that classified typing as "hands" work and managerial and professional duties as "head" work—a crucial division that we will hear more about in the next chapter. This division has been debated and evaluated for the past thirty years, but it is still around. Many of the people who are caught up in it argue that it often results in sending the same work down to the pool again and again because the division causes communication breakdowns. Juliet Webster, a sociologist who has studied clerical work, described one group of British typists, who when dictation tapes were sent to them acted out their frustration this way:

> If they said "er," we put "er" in.... So some of them came back and were furious about this and said, "This is absolute rubbish." We said, "Well, that is what you dictated, so we typed it." They wouldn't admit that they had done it.... And they do. They are really bad. They say "Oh no, typist," so we typed "Oh no, typist." They didn't like that at all.[9]

Today centralized typing or word-processing pools are no longer in management vogue because this work is being done by the professional or administrative workers who originated it. Or, as we saw in chapter 1, the high-volume document processing not done by professionals is being shipped to countries with lower wages. This outsourcing of work, however, does not solve the problems raised by the British typists and many others who have pointed out the "invisible" or tacit skills that back-office people use to decode and understand what the document is supposed to say. But during the heyday of pools—the 1960s, 1970s, and most of the 1980s—they created the framework for routinizing many tasks, such as form letters and data-entry work. And, not incidentally, the pool and back-office form of work organization played a major role in the way new office equipment was designed, because it reinforced management's belief that work needed to be divided and routinized before new technology could be effectively introduced.

Slicing Computer Operations from Programming

In the 1950s computer programming was a brand-new field, touted as the up-and-coming occupation and stereotyped as a "man's occupation," yet it had not started out that way. During the Second World War, when the first experimental computer (called the ENIAC) was developed, women were employed as "computers," a new occupation established to do what we now call programming. The recruitment of men into the field started as computer manufacturers and large companies, lacking a large enough pool of already trained applicants and faced with the fact that after the war women were being encouraged to leave professional jobs, lured mathematicians by offering them high pay and a great deal of job freedom. But this phase only lasted from the mid-1950s through the mid-1960s. After that, the demand for programmers and the paucity of workers with a science education (computer science programs did not appear until the late 1960s) meant that the math qualifications—and therefore presumably male-oriented qualifications—were often ignored. In fact, during the Vietnam War, when men were in relatively short supply in the labor market, women began to enter the field in small but noticeable numbers. The need for math and science qualifications proved essential only for the comparatively small handful of programmers who worked on scientific systems.

By the 1960s the bulk of the computer industry was moving in the direction of business-oriented applications, although it remained a field that was overwhelmingly male. The history of computer work doesn't necessarily parallel the clerical field, but there are some interesting similarities in the way computer operations were separated from programming and made into a back-office function. As with clerical work, this division of programming labor, which later extended to other programming functions, was aimed at cutting labor costs and managing workers more closely.

In the 1960s, as the demand for programmers grew, programmers had their choice of jobs, leaving managers to complain about the programmers' freewheeling, independent spirit.[10] Indeed, many early programmers saw themselves as independent craftspeople, much like the image of the computer "hacker" today. An English sociologist described how the culture of the early programmers collided with the corporate culture:

Their strange work timetable and casual dress attracted criticism. The programmers also disrupted company rules about clocking on and off. This, together with the reward their market position afforded them at such a comparatively young age, created problems within the company status system.[11]

But it wasn't just their clothing or uncorporate-like behavior that bothered management. These problems were manifestations of the fact that programmers had control over what they did. A computer programmer working in 1977 fondly recalled his job in the preceding era:

I remember that in the 1950s and early 1960s, I was a jack-of-all-trades. As a programmer I got to deal with the whole process. I would think through a problem, talk to the clients, write my own code, and operate the machine. I loved it—particularly the chance to see something through from beginning to end.[12]

By the mid-1960s, these "jacks-of-all-trades" didn't fit into the increasingly compartmentalized corporate structure. The first step that management took to gain control over the programming workforce was to divide the conceptual work of programming from the more physical tasks of computer operations. Although this division was put into effect in the aerospace industry in the mid-1950s and was subsequently used by companies that had defense contracts, it wasn't until the mid-1960s that it spread elsewhere. By 1965, when IBM began installing the general-purpose System 360, both the more expensive hardware (a large mainframe computer) and the easier-to-use software (an operating system that could be controlled through commands rather than operators working switches), gave upper and middle managers room to begin enforcing the separation of programming from operations. Operators were to stay in the "machine room" tending the computer, while programmers were to sit upstairs and write the instructions. Those of us in the field at the time remember feeling that a firm division of labor had been introduced almost overnight. It was many years before it was effective, however, because, as with the division between back- and front-office tasks, work did not flow smoothly across the physically divided workforce. Programmers who were used to operating the

A computer operations room, late 1960s. [IBM Archives]

computer in order to test programs found it difficult to explain, through written instructions, what had to be done. And operators, much like typists in back-office pools, were blamed for mistakes they couldn't even ask questions about. The division between programming and operations further divided workers and sliced up tasks that could, at least theoretically, have been controlled by bureaucratic principles.

Entering the Computer Age

Commentators in the 1950s and 1960s were full of enthusiasm for what most observers saw as a revolutionary new era. Information was portrayed as the key to knowledge and power—something that could be available to all. Television, the new magic eye into people's homes, provided advertisers with huge audiences that appeared to be delighted with the advantages of the new technology. And chief among the so-called wonders of the age was the computer.

A Short Early History of Computing

1830s   Charles Babbage and Lady Ada Lovelace work on the design for an "analytical" engine that becomes the basis for later computers. Babbage thinks that division of labor and mechanization can be applied to mental as well as manual tasks. He becomes known as the father of modern computers; Ada Lovelace, the first programmer, later has the programming language ADA named after her.

1890   Herman Hollerith is commissioned to design a system for tabulating the census. He comes up with the 80-column punched card, the basis for the current standard for turning characters and numbers into electronic bytes of information. The 80 columns served as the standard for computer screen displays until the 1990s.

1944–45   The first electronic computer, the ENIAC, is a huge room full of vacuum tubes. It is designed to calculate ballistic trajectories for bombs dropped from airplanes. Grace Hopper, a U.S. Navy officer, is head of the programming team.

1950   Remington Rand, which has moved from guns to typewriters, delivers a UNIVAC computer to the government to use in processing the census.

1954   General Electric becomes the first private company to install a computer. It is used for payroll processing.

1959   The second generation of computers is introduced. They use transistors instead of vacuum tubes and are considerably smaller and faster than their predecessors. COBOL and FORTRAN, easier-to-use programming languages, come into use.

1965   Third-generation computers, using integrated circuits, are introduced. Programming for businesses begins to take off and with it a growing occupational category: computer programmer.

The first computer was developed to calculate ballistic trajectories for bombing raids at the end of the Second World War. This massive machine, made up of huge vacuum tubes, was seen more as a marvel than as a prototype for a new computer industry. In the early 1950s, a few machines were leased to the government and to large corporations, but they were designed primarily for scientific "number-crunching," and were not viewed as essential for business. Certainly their huge size (taking up 100-foot-long rooms) and comparatively unreliable performance (vacuum tubes, like lightbulbs, burn out with use) did not make them seem like the wave of the future.

In 1959, a second generation of computers was introduced that used transistors rather than vacuum tubes, making the machines somewhat smaller and more reliable (they still required huge rooms and power supplies, however). They had the advantage of using programming languages like FORTRAN and COBOL, which were developed for them, making it easier for more people to code programs. They were in turn replaced, after 1965, by the third generation of computers, which used integrated circuits. It was these machines that finally ushered in the more widespread use of mainframe computers and prompted computer manufacturers and corporations to develop standardized software tools to be used with them.

The standardization and division of labor that were the mainstays of corporate organization also provided the principles on which the new computer programs were designed. At first, the software applications developed for these computers were custom designed for each company. They generally replicated well-defined tasks, such as calculating payroll deductions and printing inventory lists. If the tasks and procedures in a particular business or area were not already defined, the systems development process called for standardization before computerization began. In this way company after company developed codes and procedures for making processes like payrolls more routine. Indeed, functions that weren't ripe for routinization didn't fit into the programming mold. The 1957 film *Desk Set* is a good example of what happens when systems analysts try to routinize work without really understanding it. The film featured a librarian (played by Katharine Hepburn) and a computer efficiency expert (Spencer Tracy) hired to automate the library staff. In the end, the computer Tracy installs blows up, unable to keep up with the enormous knowledge and skill that Hepburn and her librarians had been using in their work.

This Hollywood version of the result of installing computers was meant to calm workers' fears about losing jobs through automation. But meanwhile, most companies followed the path of cutting departments and cutting jobs into smaller pieces and then assigning programmers to write programs for these increasingly standardized tasks, rather than try to automate entire departments.

This design process, like corporate processes in general, was not without its problems. In 1965, Robert Boguslaw, a systems analyst and critic, attempted to challenge the focus on standardization and routinization. Trying to reach an audience of system developers and managers and referring to computer system developers as the "new utopians," he wrote:

> And so it is that the new utopians retain their aloofness from human and social problems presented by the fact or threat of machined systems and automation. They are concerned with neither souls nor stomachs. People problems are left to the after-the-fact efforts of social scientists.[13]

But such warnings, like warnings about the pernicious effects of the increasing division of labor and misgivings about bureaucratic conformity, went unheeded. Computer applications continued down a path that supported the management objective of dividing labor and lowering costs. In this way, there were programs developed to separate those who keypunched data from those who entered it on forms, to separate customer relations specialists from clerical workers doing the record keeping, and so on.

The 1950s and 1960s were the beginning of the information age—the growth of business and government, and the enormous accumulation of paperwork and information. In this period, management planning focused primarily on job reorganization and the introduction of isolated pieces of office equipment. Although computers were a much talked about highlight of the period, very little computerization actually took place. Rather, this was a period of preparing for it. But in the next decade, as the volume of work increased and the labor costs, from management's perspective, skyrocketed, automation came to be considered as applicable to the office as it was to the factory.

By 1973, when the U.S. government study called *Work in America* was published, the bubble seemed to have burst on the golden future of automation and work. The report, which included a section entitled "White-Collar Woes," documented that many workers—including professionals, managers, technical workers, and clericals—were dissatisfied with their jobs because their work had been cut up into pieces and put into routine parcels, as if it were factory work. The next chapter looks at how this process, which began in the 1950s and 1960s, accelerated in the 1970s.

3. The 1970s:
The Office as the Factory of the Future

> The office today, where work is segmented and authoritarian, is often a factory. For a growing number of jobs, there is little to distinguish them but the color of the worker's collar: computer keypunch operations and typing pools share much in common with the automobile assembly line.
>
> —*Work in America,* 1973[1]

While office work in the 1970s looked a lot like office work in the 1960s, there was much going on behind the scenes that would make office work more predictable and therefore easier to code into computer programs. This would not be a simple process. *In The Coming of the Post-Industrial Society,* Daniel Bell, a well-known social scientist, coined the term "information society" to refer to the importance of computer-backed data processing.[2] But management theory held that work in the information society required a great deal of mental processing, making it difficult to codify and simplify work that was done inside of people's heads.

This was a decade of isolating people, tasks, and jobs, essentially separating the "head" of information work from the "hands" of data processing. More and more tasks, particularly those in clerical areas and in the back offices, were being treated like manual work. Data processing by definition dealt with information that had been coded and cut up into bits of data. The factory assembly line had accomplished something similar in the early part of the century, when craft workers who used skill and knowledge to make things were replaced by assembly-line workers whose rhythm of work was routinized and speeded up to fit in with automation.

Here we will first take a look at how office work was done, followed by a description of how and why computer programs were designed to fit this pattern. In the offices of large corporations in the 1970s, closed rooms lined the building's window walls, with an open space in the middle for secretaries and clerical staff. Managers, analysts, and other professionals, depending on their status within the company hierarchy, had the windowed offices. A telephone was usually the only piece of equipment on their desks. In the center, the clerical workers' metal desks marched row on row, lit by the harsh glare of overhead fluorescent lights. Each of these desks had a protruding "L" extension where an electric typewriter sat, along with a telephone and maybe some Dictaphone equipment. Most corporate and government front offices looked like this through the early 1980s. A good example of how this pre-computer office looked can be seen in the film 9 to 5, which starred Dolly Parton as a secretary, Lily Tomlin as an office manager, and Jane Fonda as a new assistant.

In the 1970s, there was rarely more than one computer in any organization or, for the larger organizations, in any one division. These mainframe computers were expensive to buy or lease and very costly to maintain. In 1976, for example, a medium-sized computer cost about $360,000 for the hardware alone, while software development costs and operations ran to many times that amount.[3] And this was a machine that had far less storage capacity and was slower than a desktop computer today.

In some offices, mainframes were connected by wires to "dumb terminals," essentially monitors with attached keyboards that had no computing capacity of their own. The use of these terminals for data-entry work followed the pattern established for clerical work in the 1960s: data entry was treated as routine work, and was, from upper management's point of view, pushed out of sight and almost out of mind.

The first word processors were introduced in the 1970s. These "stand-alone" machines were designed to speed up typing and error correction, and also included shortcuts for deleting words and letters and specialized keys for "Saving" and "Printing." They were thus not so much computers as souped-up typewriters with some electronic functions built in. The people who used them were once again named after the machines—word processors.

Word-processing machines required new skills, and many typists viewed them as a way to upgrade routine work. Some secretaries were able to use their knowledge of word processing as a stepping-stone to better pay, but for clerical workers whose work had already been routinized, word processing merely replaced the old typing pool. By placing the machines in the back office, management treated the workers who were using them as routine processors, cutting short the possibility of turning word processing into an upwardly mobile career ladder.

At the same time, insurance-claim processors, credit-card clerks, and other back-office workers were moved into their own departments—often deep in the basement of an office building or off in a separate, low-rent building, where they were even more crammed together than workers in front-office clerical areas. The pattern of sending jobs and people off was, from management's perspective, a prerequisite for developing computer programs. As we will see in later chapters it was also a prelude to sending work to subcontractors in other parts of the world.

Processing Data: The Factory Model

During the 1970s, mainframe computers became a fact of organizational life. Most of the "bugs," or programming quirks, in the mainframe operating systems had been ironed out and companies were beginning to develop applications that could handle large volumes of transactions. Insurance companies, banks, airlines, securities firms, and government agencies had high volumes of data and a large amount of repetitive work, characteristics that made them candidates for computer processing. The majority of applications were run as "batches," meaning that masses of data were accumulated and processed at periodic intervals—once a day for a bank, for example, or once a week for a payroll.

Standard bureaucratic management practices were used in supervising the development of software programs to do this work. Systems analysis—the process of designing programs—reflected both its engineering roots in Operations Research during the Second World War and managerial

Keypunch operators
prepare data cards.
Keypunch machines
were used well into
the 1970s.
[IBM Archives]

antecedents in isolating problems and separating tasks. The emphasis was on managing quantitative information—taking so-called raw data and turning it into numbers that management could review and accountants could record. This was a continuation of the management practices of the 1960s that emphasized standardization—in this case, simplifying and "rationalizing" information into standard chunks of data. The combination of routinizing tasks and standardizing data led to computer systems that recorded only routine transactions, such as accepting or rejecting insurance claims, processing payrolls at regular intervals, and filling flight reservations by destination. This essentially replicated the routine processing done by factory assembly lines.

Critics of what has come to be called the rationalistic version of system development argue that this type of analysis tends to develop computer programs that look at applications only from the perspective of those at the top of the organization. This top-down approach sees organizations as structures that can be formally described, reducing jobs and tasks to simple procedures.[4] In effect, turning work into a step-by-step, linear process forces

systems analysts to think in narrow pathways, where the emphasis is on isolating problems and searching for the one "right" solution. In fact, this type
of narrow systems thinking was applied to all kinds of issues in the late
1960s and 1970s. In a book entitled *Redesigning the Future: A Systems
Approach to Societal Programs,* systems analyst Russell Ackoff spelled out
the problems this approach created:

> [Computer systems fail] more often because we solve the wrong prob-
> lem than because we get the wrong solution to the right problem....
> The problems we select for solution and the way we formulate them
> depends more on our philosophy and worldview than on our science
> and technology.[5]

Viewed from the perspective of the people who are doing the day-to-day
work, computer systems more often than not appear to be solutions to the
wrong problems. Looking back, we can see that computer systems that were
designed to isolate specific tasks also further isolated and divided the labor
process throughout a firm and sometimes across an entire industry, such as
insurance. In social work agencies, for example, computer systems counted
welfare recipients and calculated "allowable" sums based on preprogrammed
formulas. This type of software moved social work further along a path that
divided it into such steps as "intake" and "maintenance," turning clients into
numbers to be processed by the system and taking skill and responsibility
away from the social workers—who were reduced to the now-familiar phrase,
"I'm sorry, I don't have anything to do with it—the computer did it." As
Ackoff pointed out, this type of change wasn't so much a result of technology but of the worldview of managers who accepted the systems approach as
gospel. In social work, the systems approach brought about lower costs
because routine processing meant that fewer social workers could handle the
same number of clients, and a larger number of clients could be rejected from
the system based on computer codes rather than human judgments.[6]

Many management analysts and consultants still argue that it was the
limitations of the technology that produced such repetitive routine processing. This seems doubtful. By emphasizing the hardware and ignoring
the human side, they ignore what was really happening. For instance, even
though computer terminals were available in the late 1960s, IBM marketed

hardware based on keypunch cards into the early 1970s. It claimed that this was because its clients had already invested in keypunch equipment and that applications based on batched keypunch cards were easier to manage. This worked as a marketing strategy for IBM, but it slowed the adaptation of more interactive or online systems, which today are the backbone of all Internet-based processing. Similarly, in the early 1970s both GE and RCA tried to get into "time-sharing" software, which would make it possible for many departments and many workers to access information on a main-frame simultaneously.[7] While this was to become the heart of most systems in the late 1970s and early 1980s, it was at first not very successful, in part because managers in large companies and government agencies didn't want to take a chance with something new, and because it didn't fit with estab-lished bureaucratic beliefs about who should have access to information. In the early 1970s, both GE and RCA had left the mainframe business, unable to compete with IBM, which was relying on its established customer base and continuing with the standard, and familiar, products. IBM's dominance of the hardware and software industry along with their reliance on "batch" data processing for their entrenched customer base, was one of the reasons why the factory model of automation won out over alternative approaches.

Indeed, contrary to popular stories, salable new technology is rarely devel-oped in people's garages and basements. Instead, it is the result of long periods of research and development and almost always comes from, or is ordered by, large companies. Sometimes, in fact, the potential of a new technology is not immediately recognized, as the following story and the box (p. 52) illustrate.

A Story of a Writing Tablet

In the spring of 1968 I was working for IBM as a programmer analyst. During a lull between projects, my manager assigned me to take part in a market analysis of a new product and I was sent up to the IBM laboratories in Yorktown, New York, to see a new "writing tablet." The tablet was the size of a piece of writing paper and about twice as thick as a pad. It could read printing or handwriting, and whatever was written on it was input into a mainframe computer for processing or storage. My assignment was to assess if this type of device would be useful for computer programmers—

They Didn't Think It Would Sell!

| In 1878 | Alexander Graham Bell began to lay out plans for a national network of telephones. The president of Western Union and Telegraph turned down an offer to buy the patent rights to the telephone. "What use could this company make of an electronic toy?" he asked. |

In the early 1950s Remington Rand built the UNIVAC computer. IBM rejected an offer to acquire the rights to this machine "because it felt that the greatest market potential for computers was in scientific rather than business applications."

In the late 1950s when the Xerox 914 copier was introduced, a major management-consulting firm predicted that the United States would need no more than 500 copiers at most.

In 1977 the chairman of Digital Equipment Corporation (DEC), the leading corporate developer of what came to be known as personal computers, stated: "There is no reason anyone would want a computer in their home."

In the mid-1990s when the U.S. Office of Technology Assessment held an open hearing on privatizing the Internet, no telephone companies participated, apparently believing that the Internet was not a priority for the telecommunications industry.

Source: Heidi Hartmann et al., eds., *Computer Chips and Paper Clips*, vol. 1 (Washington, D.C.: National Academy Press, 1986), p. 26; Greenbaum, *In the Name of Efficiency*, p. 26; Termer, "The Paradoxical Proliferation of Paper," p. 3.; Manual Castells, *The Internet Galaxy* (New York: Oxford, 2001), pp. 22 and 27.

whether they would want to code their programs on it or continue to send their written code down to the keypunch department (remember this was 1968 and there were as yet no desktop computers). And so I was sent to company offices around the country to interview programmers, managers, and supervisors. What I found was what the company expected: that programmers did not see any need for the writing tablet; they were happy to continue coding programs on paper and sending their code down to the keypunch department, or hastily keypunching their own cards when they had to test programs in the middle of the night.

The writing tablet I tried out was, according to the engineers I met, reliable up to 90 percent of the time (a claim that seems unlikely, but is nonetheless common among laboratory engineers).[8] It was ready to be tested and marketed. Why wasn't it introduced, and why did the programmers feel they didn't need it?

These questions are best answered with a continuation of the story. Much later in the summer of 1993, Apple introduced a palm-sized portable device called the Newton. The Newton was, of course, a smaller and more sophisticated version of the early writing tablet, one that not only recognizes handwriting but could send and receive wireless faxes and electronic mail, and also function as a pager. While the first Newton was notorious for its misperception of handwriting, the software has since been modified and now other manufacturers have jumped into the palm-size market with personal digital assistants (PDAs), and the like.

Palm-size computers have finally caught on, although the emphasis is more on their role in mobile communications than on their writing-recognition capabilities. Workers on the go, including everyone from package delivery services to doctors, rely on small portable devices to scratch out messages, signatures, and notes. In 2002 Microsoft introduced another chapter in the writing tablet story with a "tablet PC," a notebook-sized computer. Newer palm and notebook writing devices like the experimental writing tablet are not only limited by their technical features and problems, but by the practices of the users adapting them. While many people today use tablet features for quick notes and mobile tasks, keyboards remain entrenched because so many millions of users around the world have become accustomed to them. Reminding us that an "invention" may be there, but it will not be adopted until the conditions for its use are established.

Bureaucracy Blossoms

The factory model of work and systems development also won out because it fit with management's view of how organizations should be run. Today, when television shows on money management and magazines like *Business Week* talk about the "virtual corporation" where independent workers show their "entrepreneurial spirit," it is easy to forget that there was similar hype in the 1970s about corporate rule-based behavior. This was a period when bureaucratic practices held sway as national and multinational businesses expanded, and magazines showered praise on U.S. corporations and their managerial practices. In fact, the financial success of these companies was said to be partly the result of the efficiency of their bureaucratic approach to management.

The bureaucratic approach divided workers into departments, managed by lasagna-like layers of supervisors and managers. It also institutionalized office behavior, imposing impersonal rules for everything from proper office dress to forms of greeting. This was done through training, memos, meetings, and gearing salaries and promotions to annual or semiannual reviews that rated employees on these criteria. Many of us who worked for large organizations learned to follow one set of practices to keep our jobs and set ourselves up for promotion, while talking and acting in other ways when it wasn't being "counted." Men, for example, would put their jackets on to go down the hall, while women would slip off their flat shoes and put on a pair of heels when going off to a meeting. In bureaucratic organizations, managers did not have to resort to hard-line threats like "Do it or you're fired" because workers were supposed to "know what was expected of them" and act accordingly. According to Richard Edwards, an economist, getting workers to follow bureaucratic procedures worked like this:

> The defining feature of bureaucratic control is the institutionalization of hierarchical power. "Rule of law"—the firm's law—replaces "rule by supervisor command."...Work becomes highly stratified; each job is given its distinct title and description; and impersonal rules govern promotion. "Stick with the corporation," the worker is told, "and you can ascend up the ladder."[9]

This form of control, which relied on employees taking responsibility for their own work within a well-specified rule structure, was particularly suited to the white-collar workforce, which was in general well educated and recruited from the ranks of white, middle-class Americans who had been brought up to believe in "getting ahead." Promotions, salary raises, and status symbols like offices with windows all depended on conforming to corporate rules, or at least knowing when they could be broken.

But dissatisfaction with the bureaucratic model was also building during this period. Workers at all levels of the office hierarchy began to demand some kind of job enrichment and more control over their working conditions. One executive cited in the 1973 *Work in America* report put it this way:

> You feel like a small cog. Working there was dehumanizing and the struggle to get to the top didn't seem worth it. They made no effort to encourage your participation. The decisions were made in those rooms with closed doors.

The same reaction was apparent at the clerical level. This is how one college graduate expressed her dissatisfaction:

> I didn't go to school for four years to type. I'm bored, continuously humiliated. They sent me to Xerox school for three hours.... I realize that I sound cocky, but after you've been in the academic world ... and someone tries to teach you to push a button you get pretty mad. They even gave me a gold-plated plaque to show I've learned how to use the machine.[10]

Yet bureaucratic management is still very much alive. Business magazines may announce its death, but as anyone who works in an office knows, echoes of bureaucratic practices can be heard in today's carpeted cubicles. How did they become so well entrenched?

Divided and Almost Conquered

> The separation of hand and brain is the most decisive single step in the division of labor taken by the capitalist mode of production.
> —Harry Braver man, *Labor and Monopoly Capital*, 1974[11]

During the 1970s, division of labor within the labor process began to be debated by scholars and workers alike. The labor process is what economists refer to when they talk about how work is divided and who gets to do what. Although changes in the labor process may seem impersonal, the result of chance rather than design, they are in fact the result of the exercise of managerial control over the workplace, and particularly over its tasks and procedures.

In his groundbreaking 1974 book, *Labor and Monopoly Capital,* Harry Braverman offered an account of management's efforts to take control of the labor process. He argued that management needed to control the labor process not only in order to control costs but also in order to control workers.[12] By removing knowledge from workers—and therefore in essence taking away their skills—management creates a workforce that can be paid less, and one that is less likely to rebel and is therefore easier to control.

The changes in clerical and computer work, described in the last chapter, typified this process. These types of changes are the result of what Max Weber, an important sociologist, described as work rationalization, which meant breaking down each task into smaller and simpler steps, and creating specialized, narrow, and repetitive work procedures.

To management, the term rationalization applied to work has a positive value: by making work more "rational," it is also made more "sensible." But the use of such a positive-sounding term masks the fact that divided and specialized labor removes skills from the worker's control—something that is anything but sensible.

While many management consultants responded to the *Work in America* report by paying lip service to the need for more "humanistic" management,[14] Braverman argued that their strategies were essentially sugarcoating for rationalization, calling them a "style of management rather than a genuine change in the position of the worker."[13] This was particularly true, he said, in offices where "office rationalization has in part been taking place, in the most recent period, under the banner of job enlargement and the humanization of work." He went on to describe how consultants are called in to cut labor costs and "enhance" jobs: "In a typical case," he continued, "a bank teller who is idle when the load at the counter is light will be pressed into service handling other routine duties, such as sorting returned checks." The "human capital" school of management developed elaborate models of how training and enhanced skill would bring about a more productive workplace. But according to Braverman's analysis, work that had already been rationalized, such as back-office jobs, was not affected by this rhetoric.

To better understand the division of labor that was applied to office work in the 1970s, Braverman takes us back to Charles Babbage and Frederick Taylor, two people who had strongly advocated detailed division of labor. Babbage, known as the father of the modern computer, made the case in the 1830s that there were great labor savings to be made from increasing specialization and a more and more detailed division of labor. Babbage's emphasis on saving labor costs set in motion the scientific management movement that grew in the early part of this century.

Frederick Taylor, the turn-of-the-century guru of scientific management, did time-and-motion studies of factory work in order to separate it into small tasks that management could organize. In his *Principles of Scientific Management,* published in 1911, Taylor put forth three principles.

The first was that "the managers assume ... the burden of gathering together all of the traditional knowledge which in the past has been possessed by the workman and then classifying, tabulating, and reducing the knowledge to rules, laws, and formulae."

In order to accomplish this remarkable feat of gathering knowledge from workers and bringing it under managerial control, Taylor laid out his second principle: "All possible brain work should be removed from the shop and centered in the planning or laying-out department."

To make it all work, there was Taylor's third principle, which Braverman describes as the "use of this monopoly over knowledge to control each step of the labor process and its mode of execution."[15]

The three principles are interconnected. The attempt to take skills away from workers by removing their control over the labor process is supplemented by the separation of conception (thought) from execution (action), which leaves workers with fewer defenses against managerial control strategies, including bureaucratic corporate practices. Taylor's techniques were thus a clear attempt to separate the head from the hands.

To modern ears, Taylor's principles of turning work into a series of cut-and-dried rationalized operations sound harsh and even unworkable. Yet the bulk of office tasks, particularly those in the back offices of banks, insurance companies, credit card-processing facilities, and airlines, follow procedures that take the form of Taylor's recommendations. Indeed, today much of the work that has been outsourced to outside firms and other countries is outsourced on the basis of the work having first gone through the grinder of Taylor's principles.

There are countless examples of the application of these principles to office work. In the early 1970s, Studs Terkel interviewed a telephone solicitor whose story provides a glimpse of how today's telephone-based occupations, as well as automated telephone systems, were to develop:

> We didn't have to think what to say. They had it all written out. You have a card. You'd go down the list and call everyone on the card. You'd have about fifteen cards with person's names, addresses and phone numbers. "This is Mrs. DuBois. Could I have a moment of your time?"[16]

In the language of work rationalization, the worker who does the same task over and over again, working from a prepared script as this telephone solicitor did, is being de-skilled because she does not have a chance to use her own intelligence and knowledge. This is cheaper for the employer because, like piecework in the pre-assembly-line factory, the telephone worker is paid a low hourly wage plus a commission for each successful sale. In the telephone solicitor's case, the "dissociation" of the labor process from her skills diminished her sense of control over her work, leaving her feeling alienated. The worker in Terkel's account continued, "The supervisor would sometimes listen in. He had connections with all the phones.... If a new girl would come in, he'd have her listen to see how you were doing—to see how well this person was lying. That's what they taught you. After a while, when I got down to work, I wanted to cry."[17]

As early as the end of the eighteenth century, Adam Smith, the author of *The Wealth of Nations* and founder of modern economics, had warned that people become stifled in cut-and-dried jobs. In the nineteenth century Karl Marx argued that stifled workers would be, among other things, less productive. By the 1970s these projections were becoming as true for office work as they had been for factory production. The 1973 *Work in America* report noted that the cross-section of office employees surveyed were "producing at only 55 percent of their potential. Among the reasons cited for this was boredom with repetitive jobs.[18] Thus the separating of tasks done by the head (managers) from those done by the hands (workers) not only resulted in more boring work, but also cut down on potential productivity.

The Head and the Hands in Computer Work

Throughout the 1970s management continued making office work more routine. Yet problems arose as workers were moved around like different parts in a machine. By the end of the decade many managers were finding that it was very difficult to successfully "de-skill" office work because, among other things, they had finally recognized that skill itself was hard to define.[19] Attempts at de-skilling secretaries and receptionists often failed because managers and consultants never quite got it: they did not understand the wide range of tacit and behind-the-scenes knowledge that these workers— who were, of course, mostly women—needed in order to accomplish even such "simple" tasks as composing a letter. Furthermore, while management practice separated clerical workers into pools and tried to routinize functions like data entry, there was no clear way to measure whether this form of work organization produced more or better documents.

This was equally the case with the design of word-processing machines and software for mainframe computers. Systems analysts tried to build on the assumption that data could be routinely processed, but the people doing the work often spent a lot of time trying to get around the stumbling blocks created by these routinized systems. In one office, for example, clerks complained about a problem that was prevalent during the period: they had trouble locating customers by computer-generated account numbers—in their daily work the clerks had been used to dealing with customers by name. Like the problems caused by assigning codes to welfare recipients, preassigned codes not only interfered with the way clerks worked but also interfered with efficient service as customers found themselves standing in line or waiting on the phone for longer periods of time.

These were forerunners of the problems we as customers know today as we wait on hold for a real person to speak with when we need to find out what went wrong with our order, bill, appointment, or other document-based part of daily life.

Yet what these systems, both managerial and technical, lacked in their ability to turn office work into factory-like procedures they made up for in terms of their success in putting the stamp of managerial control over the work process. If we go back to the example of programming work discussed in the last chapter, we can see how further divisions of labor were cemented into place during the 1970s. Now it was systems analysts who were increasingly split off from programmers. The analysts, as their title implied, were expected to take on more and more of the conceptual work, while the programmers were relegated to the more routine functions—tasks that were standardized, simplified, and cut up into modules or chunks of computer code to be written.

Once again, the split was between head and hands, between the higher-paid work of systems analysis and the lower-paid and (it was assumed) more routine work of writing program code. And once again major problems arose. The programmers were to write code based on written specifications the analysts had developed in discussions with customers. But the programmers complained that the specifications missed "real world" things, like filing customers by name instead of by number, or recognizing that many payroll transactions required special handling rather than routine, "automatic" processing. Because programmers weren't able to talk to customers directly, they often found that they were coding and recoding the same programs in an unproductive attempt to make them do what was needed.

But by splitting off analytical work, programming jobs were routinized and salaries were reined in. The average starting salary for programmers remained static from 1970 to 1972, instead of increasing as it had up to that point. In 1975, a survey found that the salaries of programmers in large institutions had increased only 2 percent over the previous year, failing to keep up with inflation.[20] The routinization of programming, coupled with flatter salaries, gave management more control over the time, cost, and delivery of computer systems. This in turn set the stage for managers in the 1980s to order ready-made applications programs rather than hiring more programmers. And as we now know, this provided a jumping-off point for routine programming functions to be done by workers in many lower-waged countries around the world.

Winds of Economic Change

In retrospect, we can see how routinized and divided tasks didn't necessarily turn out better documents or provide for faster service. Indeed, the way the work was divided, and the way computer systems were designed to reinforce this division, limited office workers' skills and their ability to get the job done. Similar problems arose in corporations that, by dividing and segmenting work, became weighed down with bureaucracy, causing slower movement in the choppy waters of international trade. Daniel Bell's 1976 classic *The Coming of the Post-Industrial Society,* forecast a new information society,[21] yet the way information was processed in this period, retained the sharp characteristics of the earlier industrial period.

It is not just that management "styles" undergo change, but that any form of workplace activity—whether it comes from management or the workers—changes as external economic conditions (such as global competition) change and as internal contradictions bubble to the surface. During the 1970s, three large contradictions surfaced: centralized bureaucratic operations were hindering business expansion; the extensive division of labor and the routinization of work were leading to worker dissatisfaction and evidence that productivity was not increasing; and software based on routine and repetitive coding functions was not applicable to smaller computers or to non-routine transactions. Management theories in the 1970s had relied on two concepts that were considered central to economics— that economies of scale would bring economic success (bigger is better) and that intensive division of labor would result in faster and cheaper work activities. Both of these suppositions were to bend to the economic and political realities of the 1980s. And the move toward smaller organizations with less detailed division of labor called for different kinds of hardware and software.

4. The 1980s:
Stumbling Toward "Automated" Offices

They come in here every six months or so and reorganize us—send us
to seminars and focus groups on how important we are. Then they put
us back in our cubicles doing the same thing.

—Office worker, 1988

The terms *office automation,* the *office of the future,* and the *paperless
office* crept into the English language in the first half of the 1980s.
The office of the future was to be both automated and paperless,
with computer discs acting as the new filing system. The phrase office
automation implied the continuous and seamless processing of information, something like a factory assembly line. Yet, except for back-office functions, which, as we saw in the last chapter, had been rationalized in the
1960s and 1970s, there was very little that was "seamless" or smooth about
the automation that went on in the 1980s.

Indeed, it was a decade of contradictory predictions as well as practices.
Some social scientists and managers believed that the spread of the personal computer would put an end to de-skilling practices and herald the beginning of job enhancement and upgrading. Others argued that the incorpora-
tion of previously de-skilled work into computer software meant continued
de-skilling, and also set the stage for reductions in employment. Both were
partially right—depending on what part of the office you were looking at.

Offices in the 1980s began to look quite different from their predecessors, reflecting different forms of work organization and the introduction

of personal computers. For example, the 1988 film *Working Girl* showed an office overflowing with electronic equipment. In the opening shot Melanie Griffith, who plays a secretary to a group of securities traders, sits at a small desk that is crowded with a computer terminal (presumably connected to the stock market system) and a personal computer. In addition to looking different, skills and rules changed in the 1980s. In the film, Griffith is a secretary who crosses the class line by "breaking the rules" and using company trading knowledge in addition to her keyboarding skills. By the end of the movie, she has "made it" out of the open area of secretarial workstations into her own windowed office.

The Office of the Future?

In terms of technology, the 1980s can best be seen as broken into two parts. The front office of the first half was not much different from the front office of the 1970s, with a few personal computers added to take care of clerical functions. It was not until the second half of the 1980s that personal computers spread up through the office hierarchy, accompanied by increasingly common fax machines, voice-mail systems, and other forms of office technology.

By mid-decade many stand-alone word-processing machines had been replaced by computers. But the early "office of the future" didn't look like the safe, clean, pleasant working environment that advertisements seemed to promise. The introduction of desktop computers was rather haphazard, reflecting that managers weren't sure what they could be used for, or, in fact, where or how they should be used. In some offices, what seemed like miles of cable was run from machine to machine in a primitive attempt at networking. Many office workers complained about lack of space, and the situation only worsened as newer model PCs replaced outdated ones every eighteen months or so, leaving the older models sitting on file cabinets or stuffed awkwardly into bookcases. In addition to overcrowding, there was the serious problem of the decibel levels created by dot-matrix printers banging out printed pages. In many front offices these printers drowned out normal conversation, and the sound level in back offices was, as one word processor put it, "thunderous." While ergonomic experts (specialists who study the fit between people and machines) recommended muffling the printer noise, little attention was paid to where the new PCs were placed, particularly when they were being used by clerical workers. And while carbon paper was getting to be a thing of the past, workers' hands were not necessarily any cleaner, because changing ribbons on the printers was a messy and time-consuming task. It wasn't until the later part of the decade that devices to buffer sound, like hoods and underpads, were widely introduced, along with ink cartridges instead of printer ribbons.

By the second half of the 1980s, computers had moved onto the desks of managers and professionals in most professions—with the exception of law firms and government offices, which were slow to jump on the PC bandwagon. Green and amber text flickered on screens (computer makers were still experimenting with which colors were easiest to see) everywhere. At first, managers routinely complained that they had to rely on their secretaries to explain "how the thing worked." One middle-level manager voiced a concern that was repeated by many: "I didn't even know how to turn it on. And of course I didn't know how to type. All this 'Hit Shift, Command, Option' stuff had me confused. I'm really dependent on [my secretary] for getting out of tough situations."

The physical layout of the office also changed. It was at this point that the use of office cubicles really caught on. Cubicles had been in use for several decades, but it was not until the 1980s that management strategists starting ordering cubicles en masse, perhaps because by then they fit in with plans for decentralizing work. At the same time, sets of cubicles fit in with the newer notion, borrowed from the Japanese management practice of a team approach. Cubicles were a physical way of more flexibly shifting workers around into different "teams," as well as meeting the objective of squeezing more people into less space at a time when real estate costs were rising rapidly. Modular offices were successfully marketed by companies like Steelcase, Inc., a large supplier of office furniture, as a lower-cost approach to office and organizational design. Cubicles, complete with partition walls in different sizes, upper and lower cabinet space, and a variety of fabric coverings provided not only some limited form of sound barriers in crowded offices, but also indicated status by their size and color.

By the end of the decade, cubicle partitions, like personal computers, were a common feature of the office. They were the physical manifestations of other changes that were taking place in the design, development, and marketing of hardware and software.

Enter the (Not Very) Personal Computer

Microcomputers, or what later came to be called personal computers or desktop computers, had been around since the 1970s, when electronics buffs bought kits in order to build their own machines. By the early 1980s, Atari, an early manufacturer of microcomputers, had produced an array of educational software, as well as games. Apple also came on the scene at this time, marketing to homes and schools.

In the office market, Wang and Xerox sold word-processing machines that included specialized hardware and built-in software. During the early part of the decade "knowing the Wang or the Xerox" was considered a strong job-hunting skill for a secretary or office assistant. In addition, although there were a number of companies that manufactured general-purpose microcomputers (as opposed to specialized machines, like Wang's word processors), there were few software programs available for them. Software companies had not yet begun mass marketing directly to businesses.

In 1982, IBM jumped into the microcomputer market by introducing its "personal computer." These were much like other computers at the time: the difference was in IBM's sales force and marketing strategy, which aimed at offices rather than homes and schools. As it had with its keypunch equipment and mainframe computers in the 1960s and 1970s, IBM used its already established corporate connections to win a foothold in the office market, telling managers that the best thing was to stay with the company they knew.

Several things went wrong, however: IBM not only misjudged what its computers would and could be used for, but in emphasizing hardware it left software, training, and work reorganization by the wayside. It was also vulnerable to being pushed out of the hardware market by lower-priced compatible computers, or "clones." Perhaps the only aspect of IBM's first move into personal computers that seemed to stick was the name PC. This was, in retrospect, a strange name since PCs were targeted at the office market in office environments where they were certainly not very personal.

The PC carried over the antiquated QWERTY keyboard design from the typewriter. In the nineteenth century, the QWERTY keyboard—named for the letters on the left side of the top row—was designed to actually slow English-language typists down so that the metal keys wouldn't stick together when they sprang up from the typewriter and struck the paper. By the early 1980s, there were over 3 million clerical workers with keyboard experience. Rather than rock the boat by introducing both computers and a redesigned keyboard, designers stuck with the typewriter format. The QWERTY keyboard is a strange reminder that technical design often follows, rather than leads the way, particularly now that there are billions of people using keyboards around the world, and most of them are not writing in English.

Although much of the history of technology focuses on hardware, it was the development of software applications in the 1980s that sparked personal computer use. The story of Visicalc, the first spreadsheet program, is widely known to early computer users. The spreadsheet was a fairly simple program that arranged numbers in rows and columns, adding up the totals and calculating percentages and averages, in a simplified version of something like today's Excel program. It was generally credited with having been the program that made professionals see the value of using computers. In particular, many accountants, auditors, and supervisors were quick to find out that they could use it to set up budgets, track sales, and keep records and statistics. Indeed, the program was, in part, so successful because users generated their own ideas for how it could be used, including things like keeping sports statistics, cooking recipes, name and address lists, and appointment calendars.[1] Spreadsheet programs like Excel and Lotus have followed the Visicalc model, and today remain near the top of the list of best-selling programs.

Word-processing software, also widely used in the early 1980s, was not so quickly adopted into managerial and professional occupations. Part of the problem was that word-processing programs were designed for secretaries, and the designers seemed to have assumed that secretaries merely input what their bosses wrote. Early word-processing programs were therefore designed for input speed rather than for formatting and editing. This was also the result of the failure of technical specialists to take seriously the "invisible skills"—like rewording and editing—used in what was considered women's work. WordStar, for example, the first big-selling word-processing program for the PC, had hopelessly complex sets of commands (using the Shift, Control, and Function keys in different combinations), combined with the next-to-impossible-to-remember letters that were used with the function keys (like "Ctrl-G" for erasing a character). But its major flaw was that it separated supposedly routine functions like entering text from more editorial ones like formatting and rearranging text—the classic separation of head from hands that was discussed in the last chapter.

Coordinate and Control

Whether one reads Marx or conservative capitalist economists, management's function is to coordinate and control divided labor, pulling together various departments of head and hand work. By the end of the 1970s, it had become clear to management that the extensive division of labor used in most large organizations was leading to worker dissatisfaction, no reported gains in productivity, and decreased control over quality. According to the business press, the United States, the leader in postindustrial development, was now looking at what was being called the "Japanese challenge." Many management experts began to recommend that instead of further centralization, companies should begin to *decentralize*—spread out coordination and operations functions. It was also suggested that there would be fewer coordination problems if there were less division of labor and more collapsing of job titles.[2] It was not that management objectives had changed: the basics of reducing labor costs and increasing productivity were still paramount. But the underlying assumption behind large, centralized workplaces—that they should be organized around "economies of scale"—was being challenged by decentralized, scaled-down production strategies. The realization that Japan might be succeeding with smaller-scale manufacturing, particularly in auto production, turned management's eyes in that direction.

Not everyone agreed that keeping up with the Japanese was the correct solution. For one thing, it was an open question whether Japan's decentralized "lean" factory production strategies were appropriate for U.S. offices. For another, it was not clear that there was a known strategy for fitting job design together with technology. In a study commissioned by the U.S. Congress, the Office of Technology Assessment found that simply moving organizational pieces around did not work. They had this to say about introducing computers into workplaces:

> Where organizational issues like job redesign and workflow restructuring have not been properly managed, organizational costs can more than offset productivity gains expected from new technology. A number of firms were demonstrably worse off with automation than they were without it, at least in the short run.[3]

In other words, organizational restructuring and office automation had to be planned together and made to fit together. And there was no existing model, Japanese or otherwise, that showed how this should be done.

Throughout the 1980s, the traditional reliance on centralized, rationalized policies existed side-by-side with the newer decentralized operations; back-office operations generally followed the 1970s practice of centralization and rationalization, while front-office functions, particularly professional and analytical jobs, were more likely to be decentralized. Yet both remained built on the historical base of bureaucratic rule-based practices.

Management theorists argued that in order to make decisions swiftly in an expanding global market, the threads of bureaucratic control had to unravel, along with the fabric of hierarchical chain of command. Management experts today like to say that U.S. companies should have gotten rid of bureaucratic overhead and downsized sooner. But even in restructured organizations, the essence of bureaucracy—its reliance on self-disciplined workers who have internalized corporate rules—remains intact, as have the control systems upper management developed in the heyday of corporate and governmental bureaucracy. Indeed, managerial emphasis in the early twenty-first century on entrepreneurial workers working for themselves and jumping professionally from project to project stems in part

from the expectation that workers have already internalized corporate practices and can discipline themselves.

Networks and "Users"

In 1980 virtually all of corporate computing power was in mainframes, and in 1987, 95 percent of corporate computing power was in
desktop PCs.

—*Forbes,* 1993[4]

The shift from mainframes to PCs brought with it technical changes that
reflected managerial policy about workplace reorganization.[5] An interme-
diate step between the mainframe and the PC was the minicomputer, which
also came into widespread use in the 1980s. Minicomputers, which cost less
than mainframes, also took up less space, were easier to operate, and were
important in setting up networks. They became the workhorses in the move
to decentralize corporate departments and their computer services. This
change gave departmental managers and computer center directors more
say about the work that could be carried out within their realms; it also gave
more workers access to computers and potentially gave them greater access
to information as well.

Some minicomputers are still around as network servers, but they were
soon matched in speed and storage capacity by PCs. By the end of the
1980s, minicomputers were being replaced by high-capacity PCs acting as
file servers (workstations that function as switching stations) in coordinat-
ing Local Area Networks (LANs). As one technical analyst put it, "People
don't have to beg for information anymore." LANs fit the bill by fitting into
flatter organizations that could, in theory at least, support decentralized
decision making.

But while LANs in theory solved the problem of how to spread information through large decentralized organizations, in practice managers
and technical specialists had to deal with a technological Tower of Babel:
too many pieces of hardware couldn't be used together, while protocols
(hardware and software standards) lagged far behind. Software, particularly the operating systems that direct the flow of information between and

among computers and input/output devices, lacked industry-wide standards, making it very difficult to share files and information. For much of the decade, management philosophy, workplace practices, and technical achievement were out of sync.

Many office workers who began using computers in this period remember the frustration of trying to get a disk from one computer to work on another, or simply trying to get something printed out from someone else's printer. Rush jobs, a common office phenomenon, often ran into the evening as files got lost in temporary wired-together networks, or disappeared due to "disk error." This was time-consuming as well as frustrating, with clerical workers, professionals, and managers often saying that doing something on the computer took more time than it would have by hand.

Systems analysts and directors of newly emerging Management Information Systems (MIS) departments tried to get around these hardware and software problems by designing new systems from scratch. But here too there were missteps and missed cues because they often focused on the wrong problem. For the developers of computer systems, the decade was one of discovering the "user," the name given by computer specialists to those who used the machines.[6] A focus on user issues began to dominate computer management and system development literature, but most books, articles, and seminars addressed the issue of how to "integrate the user" into the system, not how the system could serve the user. In the 1970s, development literature focused too heavily on routinized systems and rationalized procedures, failing to acknowledge people. While computer systems analysts were beginning to actually look at people, they were still ignoring how those people worked.[7]

The goal of designing "idiot-proof" systems (computer programs that made it almost impossible to hit the wrong function key) was another theme of managers and system developers in this period. Particularly in the area of custom-designed applications for back-office operations, systems analysts were warned to keep the number of steps down to a minimum so that any "idiot" could learn to use the program—missing the point that much back-office work involved the invisible work of making decisions and setting priorities.

Furthermore, most software was tested in controlled laboratories rather than actual workplaces. This meant that designers missed the complexity of real-life work, where several tasks are taken on at once. Lab testing can't catch common issues, such as the fact that we may be answering the phone at the same time we are responding to a "prompt" from a software application. If, for example, the prompt asks if we should save a file, and we hit the Enter key instead of typing "Yes," the result can be many hours of lost work. Similar problems still remain in the software industry for most applications and websites are *still* tested on users in controlled settings rather than in the rich and complex multitasking environments people work in.[8]

The Art of System Development

In hindsight, the idea that idiot-proof and lab-tested systems could actually be effective seems shortsighted, yet this notion dominated system development in the 1980s and still hovers around today. Indeed, hardware and software problems of the sort just described were more a failure to recognize actual work practices than they were technical failures. To better understand how this happened, it is useful to know a little more about the theory and practice of system development.

Systems development literature, including widely known books by such authors as Edward Yourdon and Tom DeMarco, called on system designers to mimic the physical sciences by being "objective" and "isolating the problem." These experts maintained that the systems approach must be one

> that breaks large complex problems into smaller less complex problems and then decomposes each of these smaller problems into even smaller problems, until the original problem has been expressed as some combination of many small solvable problems.[9]

These systems practices of breaking down problems into small and smaller units are not aimed at designing systems that real people can use in real situations. The consultants' approach looks at *information flow* rather than social relationships, *problems* instead of workplace situations, personnel-file *skill descriptions* rather than tacit knowledge, and rule-based procedures over on-the-job experience.[10] Essentially, real work is made invisible by these procedures.

What these approaches lack in originality and human orientation they make up for in cost control as well as control over the management of information. As in the 1970s, the main complaint of the managers who were buying programming services was that custom-designed software was too expensive and took too long to be delivered. The structured systems approach—the name given to the methods used by Yourdon and others—promised to deliver more predictable software on time and within budget. The "bottom line" therefore took priority over finding ways to develop computer systems that would better fit the work.

Take the case of data-entry clerks who enter health insurance claim information. The supposedly idiot-proof processing systems they use have been designed to accept or reject claims on the basis of the codes they enter. Although a fair amount of judgment goes into entering and assigning codes, with clerks often having to refer to medical reference lists or call doctor's offices, many insurance computer systems have been designed with the assumption that entering codes is a routine function, and one that can be speeded up by designing data-entry screens that call only for codes, with no further explanations. By ignoring work practices and instead focusing on units of data (like medical codes), system analysts not only get the systems designed and programmed faster but they also speed up the work of the claims processors. The result is a system that rejects more claims than it accepts—the bottom of the bottom line, because the insurance company can pay out less to customers.

Automating and "Informating" Offices

In *The Age of the Smart Machine*, Shoshana Zuboff, a well-known social scientist, argued that centralized, rationalized policies would lead to computer systems that would be "automating" the workplace, while decentralized enhancement schemes could lead to systems that would be "informating" work. Zuboff and others are strong advocates of the informating strategy, which they believe, when combined with managerial decisions on job design, results in better and more meaningful jobs:

While it is true that computer-based automation continues to displace the human body and its know-how (a process that has come to be known as deskilling), the informating power of the technology simultaneously creates pressure for a profound re-skilling.[11]

Informating, in Zuboff's view, would mean using information technology to enhance and upskill, giving responsibility and knowledge back to those doing the work—in other words, using new forms of work organization and newer office technologies to set back the clock on rationalization and de-skilling.

But while this faith in upskilling did filter up to front-office and professional jobs, most work that had already been divided remained automated and in the 1980s was either relegated to isolated parts of the building or hidden behind cubicle partitions. Why was this so? If social science, management policy, and computer technology could have been used to bring about more integrated, re-skilled jobs, why was this more talked about than implemented?

One answer to questions like this lies in the contradiction between informating practices that would humanize work and management policies that are aimed at lowering labor costs. In the 1980s, the movement to lower labor costs took on new momentum and, as a result, work was further divided or recombined so that it could be done with fewer workers. The newer policies were coated in the rich language of "enhancing human resources," making it seem that much was being done to improve skills and jobs. But, as we will see in the next chapter, employment figures and salaries in the 1990s illustrate that management continued the rationalization of tasks and jobs that had already been standardized and simplified, while at the same time identifying new tasks and functions (like paraprofessional and technical jobs) that could be molded into standardized forms. By the end of the 1980s, more reliable software was being developed to reintegrate previously rationalized tasks and standardized services. And a new angle was pursued to combine work organization with software. This was to create standard products and services. In this newer round of cost-cutting, the emphasis was not only on making workers and software more predictable, but on carving up services so that they too would be standardized and predictable.

Redefining Products and Services

There is an adage in economics that says, "It is not possible to greatly increase the number of haircuts a barber can give in an hour." In other words, it is difficult to raise productivity in the service sector. On the surface, this might seem to be true, but if the definition of either service or product is changed, then it is possible to increase production. For instance, McDonald's changed the meaning of meal production by mass-producing the new "service" of fast food, thus making it possible to produce more hamburgers in an hour. In fact, hairdressers standardized and simplified hairstyles in the early 1970s when they introduced the cut-and-blow-dried look—which meant they were able to produce more haircuts per hour.

In the 1980s, this strategy of redefining services was done in banks, insurance companies, airlines, hotels, and government agencies. Like Henry Ford's Model T and Wonder Bread's sliced loaf, products in the service sector would be predetermined and measured so that they could be produced faster and for less. Essentially this management strategy follows a standard practice of capitalist economics—that of turning everything into commodities that can then be sold in expanding markets. In the office sector, this was particularly true for back-office functions.

Automated telephone response systems, now a fixed part of life, were introduced in the later part of the 1980s and are a classic example of a standardized and rationalized service that was turned into a sellable product by software and telecommunication firms. In the 1980s version, when a customer called an office, he or she was given a range of preselected options. Each option button puts one through a defined channel to a person doing a specialized function. The customer service representatives who performed these specialized functions were often located in an office far from headquarters. Their jobs had already been routinized and standardized to follow scripts. In *The Electronic Sweatshop,* Barbara Garson quotes an airline reservation agent who has been given a script to sell airline tickets:

> There's AHU, that's After Hang Up time. It's supposed to be fourteen seconds. It just came down to thirteen. But my average is five seconds AHU, because I do most of the work while the customer's still on the phone. There's your talk time, your availability, your occupancy—

An early Personal Computer in 1981. [AP Photo]

that's the percent of time you're plugged in—which is supposed to be 98 percent.[12]

Talking to an actual customer representative today, of course, requires pressing one's way through the chain of telephone buttons and recorded messages, and constantly being redirected to the company's website. But the telephone representative, whether in the country you are calling from or somewhere else in the world, is following a script similar to those outlined in Garson's scenario.

As with industrial production, not all products and jobs can be easily rationalized. In banking, for example, many new services, such as variable-rate mortgages and refinancing options, require customized, in-person attention from customer service representatives. Mortgage information can be built into a database, but it is up to the bank representatives to explain and "sell" it to the customer. And in the airline industry in the 1980s, travel agents still provided a fuller range of nonstandard services than the airlines did, although with an increasing array of package tours being offered as more standardized products. Some of these new services came under the knife of rationalization in the 1990s, this time under the banner of reengineering, as we will see in the next chapter. And others, like booking flights and travel, got boiled down to a series of programs and databases that are now linked to travel websites.

Speeding up the pace of work was an *intended* consequence of standardizing services and software. Up until this period, professional work had not been timed or monitored because it was assumed to require thinking, and common sense held that thinking could not be measured. But this too was to change in the 1980s. "Everyone expects everything yesterday" became as common a complaint among professional and managerial staff as it had been among clerical workers. In part this was due to the proliferation of fax machines, voice mail, and software applications like databases and spreadsheets that were expected to produce results "at the touch of a button." But it was also the result of changing the definition of professional work to bring it more in line with measured results and standardized services. An analyst with a municipal agency put it this way:

> At first they wanted more reports from me. You know, "plug in" the statistics and crank out the graphs. Then it turned out that longer reports were expected. And of course the reports have to be typed perfectly and be beautiful.

The analyst, like many professional workers, found that in order to get the work done, he had to work longer and harder—an intensification of work that was to take on monumental proportions in the 1990s.[13] He was also experiencing the clericalization of professional work that continues today, as most professionals and managers are expected to do their own word processing and handle their phones and e-mail.

In clerical jobs, what seemed at first to be little changes produced tremendous increases in the pace of work. These small changes included no longer having to get up to put a piece of paper in the typewriter, file a document, mail a letter, or look up information in a manual. In addition, having keystrokes counted sped up the pace for many back-office clerical workers. By the second half of the decade office workers reported serious physical problems, such as carpal tunnel syndrome, resulting from repetitive motion at the keyboard, and eye strain and severe headaches from staring at a computer screen all day.[14]

Another consequence of standardization was management's ability to move work around to wherever wages were less. In the office sector it was typified by the proliferation of call centers for everything from bank balances to software technical support. Translating complex, in-person services into the more routine procedural steps of telephone "scripts" meant that this kind of work could be moved anywhere and done at any time. It also meant that corporate headquarters, which had moved from the central cities to the suburbs in the 1970s, were able to move further away from the reach of inner-city and minority workers in the 1980s.[15] And all of these issues were deeply intertwined with continuing discussions about skill.

To Skill or Be De-skilled, Is That the Question?

In the 1970s, Harry Braverman's critical analysis of rationalized work processes led to scholarly and workplace discussions about the negative effects of de-skilling. In the 1980s, these dialogues continued in the form of "skills debates," where some argued that newer forms of work organization and technology could bring about the rise of the "knowledge worker"—a person who could use all sorts of information technology.[16] Knowledge work was the epitome of upgraded and integrated work, with higher skill expectations and more challenging job content. But the dark side of knowledge work could be seen in the still increasing number of support staff jobs. Although people were using more information technology and taking on more responsibility, it was not reflected in rising wages or in higher status or promotional opportunities.

Just as centralized and decentralized corporate structures existed side by side, so too did jobs in which skill was being removed coexist with upskilled or "knowledge worker" jobs. To better understand this process of polarized skill, it is useful to take a look at the broader aspects of skill, beginning with an understanding of how managers plan job design and work organization.

Tasks and responsibilities are two aspects of what economists call *job content,* and they change as work is reorganized. In this period, managers and consultants advocated broadening job content, which brought with it increasing skill requirements. An example of this can be found in *Brave New Workplace,* where Robert Howard recounts a "what if" scenario in a large bank. Before work reorganization, one letter-of-credit department worker said of his job, "You used to do one job continuously. You could go a little crazy it was so boring."[17] Management hired a consultant who suggested that rather than using computers as if the department was a factory assembly line, work could be organized differently. Howard describes the consultant's concept this way:

> What if, instead of dividing up the tasks in the back office, they were woven together into a coherent whole? ...And what if technology was used to support this redesign of work, rather than simply freezing the inefficient organization already in place?[18]

Some would see the suggested reorganization as the new humanistic management style, integrating tasks and proposing job enhancement, or upskilling. Indeed, it was done in the early 1980s, a time when government deregulation was pushing banks to explore new markets. This in turn called for some new products and services, new computer systems, and a reorganized labor process, which some saw as job enhancement. But the changes also contained another characteristic, one that was to become all too common: "By simplifying and "cleaning up" the work process, the department would require fewer workers and labor costs would plummet."[19]

The results of these strategies were unfortunately all too predictable. Since women and minorities did a high percentage of the work that was "automated out," they bore the brunt of this change. In 1982, for example, over 80 percent of the more than 18 million clerical workers were women. Of these, the three job categories with more than 20 percent minority workforces—keypunch operators, mailroom clerks, and file clerks—were not only the lowest paid but were among the first to be cut.[20]

Skill is closely linked to job content. In the late 1980s, skills were integrated into computer systems at all levels within organizations, but with noticeably different effects. Shoshana Zuboff, linking skill with her idea of "informating" work, explains how computer systems could be used to increase skill levels in clerical positions:

> Activities that had once been extracted from the professional domain and rationalized in lower level jobs could now be reintegrated with those higher level positions. For example, bank workers could interact directly with the database, perform analyses, and develop ideas. The remaining clerical positions would take on a quasi-professional status, requiring information management and business knowledge.[21]

The scenario Zuboff sketched came to be called the "professionalization of clerical work," the flip side of professionals getting to do "clericalized" work. A problem with it, however, is that it is implemented only when managers (or the army of consultants they hire) are able to show that overall labor costs are decreasing and that the remaining people are producing more. Another problem with this more rosy skill-enhancement scenario is the fact that the invisible dimensions of a clerical worker's skill—the harder to quantify, more tacit aspects of the job—rarely get included in job descriptions or evaluations.[22] Thus when it comes time to make clerical work more professional, workers may be expected to perform with more skills, but won't necessarily be compensated for the new knowledge and skill they bring to the job. As we will see, this is particularly true of computer skills.

The 1980s were a time when there were a number of organizational and technical alternatives to rationalized, bureaucratic work practices. Yet these possible choices faded as management reined in labor costs and used office technology to further control both costs and work processes. In 1985, Congress's Office of Technology Assessment conducted a series of case studies of different industries in order to study changes in office technology, employment patterns, job training, organizational structures, job content, and skill. They argued that it wasn't the technology that was shaping changes in skill and job content, but rather the choices that were being made.

The report, called *Automation of America's Offices,* stressed that by mid-decade changes in work were bringing about shifting power relations between management and the workforce: "These shifts in power depend less on the characteristics of the technology than on the characteristics of the organization and its management strategy."[23] Their predictions, grounded in careful analysis, pointed to changes that have since occurred. In general, they believed that the workplace developments of the early part of the 1980s would become more pronounced in the following decade. Specifically, they pointed to the increasing readiness of management to reduce labor costs by reducing back-office jobs, to limit the growth of middle-management jobs. and to spread work to part-time and temporary workers, as well as to move it out of the city and out of the country. In the 1990s, top management strategists were able to begin reengineering the workplace in order to carry out these changes more smoothly. In the next chapter we will turn to an examination of how the principles of reengineering combined organizational and technical change in order to bring about the world of work we know today.

5. The Early 1990s: Reengineering the Office

It's not that you're being fired; it's the job that's being eliminated.
—District Manager, AT&T, 1994[1]

In 1990 and 1991 a recession masked structural job shifts—shifts that were bringing about huge cuts in the number of "payroll" or full-time jobs, a compression of job titles in those that remained, and a surge in the "contingent" or "work-for-hire" workforce. These three changes were coupled with the increasingly common phenomenon of people working from home, both as "telecommuters" (on the payroll) and as self-employed freelancers. All of these changes were propelled in part by the management practice of business process reengineering. While sounding soothingly simple, business process reengineering, combined with something called Total Quality Management (TQM) was used to flatten organizational hierarchies, reorganize work processes, redefine required skills, and introduce new technologies. The corporate way of organizing work, with its job ladders and relatively secure jobs, was being rebuilt to resemble the entrepreneurial ideal—one where workers would fend for themselves. And last but not least, the restructured world of work was held in place through computer and communications networks, as well as by other now familiar varieties of office technology, which, like schemes for reorganizing work, were designed to get more work out of remaining workers.

Think back to the early 1990s. If you were working then you will remember that there were not yet computers on every desk; and to be sure women administrative assistants were more likely to use them than higher-up male executives. Networks, to the extent that they were in use, were mostly local area networks (LANs) within offices, with some limited use of e-mail in offices. While the Internet had been in use by the military and academics, there was no widespread use of the Internet in the business world, no World Wide Web (which began to catch on in 1995), few cell or mobile phones (at least not in the United States) and certainly no major use of wireless connections.

By the early 1990s, the previous effects of division of labor and work reorganization were now coupled with a recession, and with the more extensive use of technology. For workers this meant less job security and with it increased anxiety. In 1994, President Clinton's secretary of labor, Robert Reich, sounded an alarm by referring to what he called the "anxious class," which he explained was made up of "millions of Americans who no longer can count on having their jobs next year, or next month, and whose wages have stagnated or lost ground to inflation."[2] Joshua Freeman, a labor historian, noted that restructuring left "no structure to deal with the new anxiety and uncertainty."[3] Or as one corporate chief executive officer put it: "We have fewer people doing much more work, much of which is knowledge-based, and we're paying people less."[4]

By the early to mid-1990s the big stories in business magazines were, like the cover story of an issue of *Fortune* magazine, proclaiming "The End of the Job." The *Fortune* article argued that traditional employment in well-worn occupational categories was "no longer the best way to organize work," and that the traditional job was becoming a "social artifact."[5] *Business Week* jumped in saying that there was a surge in the number of workers being pushed out by waves of downsizing, forming a large pool of what it called "corporate refugees."[6] And *Time* magazine, speaking to a more general audience, reported:

> By now, these trends have created an "industrial reserve army"—to borrow a term from Karl Marx—so large that a quite extraordinary and prolonged surge in output would be required to put all its members to full-time, well-paid work.

While TV and radio talk-show culture continued to push the myth of high-tech, high-skill, high-wage jobs in its one-minute sound bites, *Time*

continued, "the white-collar layoffs are permanent and structural. These jobs are gone forever."[7]

Flexible Workers

Jobs don't change overnight. Patterns of reorganization build on prior structural changes. Following are examples of changes in the first half of the 1990s from two occupational areas discussed in earlier chapters, computer jobs and clerical work, that still employed people in more or less traditional office settings. First we will take a look at the new twists in programming work that reintegrated some programming, analysis, and management functions but resulted in the trends we saw beginning slowly in the 1980s: jobs being done by fewer people, working longer hours, and engaging in what came to be called multitasking.

In 1994, when I interviewed Jack, a project manager in the information services division of a large industrial company, he had to drag a coworker's chair into the hallway outside his cubicle so I could have a place to sit.

"There are rules about office size," he explained, "but since we moved here three years ago, the whole technical staff has been pissed off because we have too much equipment and no place to put it. There isn't even enough space for our power cords."

According to Jack the crowded conditions directly affect productivity in the office. "How is a programmer supposed to write code, for example, when he is sitting on the other side of a thin wall from a salesperson who is on the phone all day? " he said.

Jack went on to describe the big organizational shake-up his corporation was going through. "We used to have twenty levels of titles, but in 1986-1987 they jumbled them up and squeezed us into three 'career bands.'"

Like similar "broad-banding" efforts in other large organizations, Jack's division was squeezed into three broad bands, or categories: administrative/support, technical/professional, and managerial. As a project manager, he is part of the technical/professional band; management positions start higher up in the organizational chart. Middle managers were cut, as were secretaries and most support staff. Jack didn't think that the bands affected salaries much, but since it is company policy not to discuss this, he wasn't really sure. It is clear that raises are effectively smaller, however, because "they have lengthened the time between salary reviews from twelve to fourteen or sixteen months."

For Jack, a senior technical person with nine years in the company, the real change began about two years before when management began assigning each project manager more than one project at the same time. "It's not like they want us to complete a project faster," he explains, "but it's an increase in the pace of work because we are working on so many things at once."

I talked with Jack over a period of several years since that interview. He often had to work late, "pulling bugs" out of programs—those he had written and programs that he was responsible for. As a project manager, he did just about everything, from coding programs to going around with salespeople and talking to customers. Perhaps we can think of him as the 1990s equivalent of the "jack of all trades," but his range of skill didn't get him a better salary or more control over his working environment.

The work that Jack and other project managers and systems analysts do is less divided than management had, in earlier periods, believed that it should be. Instead of the assembly-line rigid division of labor tried by managers in the 1970s and the structured programming of the 1980s, the 1990s restructuring of work led to more being done with fewer people. And this could be accomplished, in part, because programming was then based on structured programming languages and standardized system development tools that were developed in the previous periods. From top management's perspective, what couldn't be done by dividing and standardizing the work could instead be accomplished by using more standardized tools, techniques, and software.

Clerical work also was changing markedly during this period. The then growing job of customer service representative is worth examining, and for this we turn to an interview I did with Sandy in 1992. What was happening to Sandy's work was fairly typical of what was happening in back offices and call centers, where tasks were being integrated into jobs that required more skill but without any increase in wages. When I visited Sandy she was sitting in a reasonably sized low-walled cubicle and was surrounded by about 350 other customer service representatives. When she stood up from her ergonomically designed chair, she had a clear view of trees and sky out through the large windows that surround the suburban building's open floor plan. She worked for an 800-line operation in a large bank.

> From the moment Sandy sits down and keys her ID number into the automated call distributor (phone system), she is online and monitored. As calls come in, she pulls up customer records on her multiwindowed screen and goes to work sorting out customer problems. Queries can range from a request for an account balance (although most of these are handled by the totally automated voice-response system) to complicated problems where Sandy needs to test her "listening skills" so that she can help the caller identify his or her concerns and unravel whatever has gone awry with the account. In addition to handling customer service calls, representatives are encouraged to sell new bank products, such as certificates of deposit, to the customers who call.
>
> Training for the job was intensive, with almost a month of full-time in-house courses and several weeks at a "training hall," where "team trainers"

listened in and talked her through each call. Team trainers, supervisors, and quality-control experts—three levels of monitors—continue to listen in to a certain percentage of her calls and give her a monthly rating on how well she is doing. She is evaluated on the number of calls handled per hour, and on a variety of quality characteristics that zero in on her level of courtesy, clarity, and accuracy in giving out information. Good ratings bring silver stars—actually silver star-shaped balloons that float over the cubicles—and a certain number of silver stars mean a cash prize. Starting pay was then a lowly $19,000 a year, but the job attracted a large number of applicants because it came with health benefits and a tuition refund plan.

Sandy calls her work "boring" and "numbing," but acknowledges that it requires a lot of skills, from listening to and counseling customers to a great deal of problem solving. She, like her coworkers, takes the computer system for granted, navigating her way through a warren of screens and windows, trying to outguess customers as to which screen they may need next.

In the late 1980s and the first half of the 1990s banks were training customers to use the call centers instead of going to their local branches, so that banks could cut down on the number of "brick and mortar positions," thereby slicing the number of tellers and branch personnel.

Telephone-based customer service work was growing in the 1990s, before call centers were routed out of the United States.[8] Customer-service call center work integrated back-office functions with front-office customer relations functions—without the in-person contact. Much of this work, like Sandy's, is subject to close monitoring, which has increasingly been built into automated telephone trees, computer systems, and websites. Productivity can be measured in ways reminiscent of factory work as workers answer an ever-increasing target number of calls per hour. And the scripted nature of the call procedure lends itself to management monitoring of how well representatives state the scripted opening and closing remarks, and how completely they inform the customer about each transaction. This couldn't have been accomplished if each part of a phone call and each aspect of bank work had not first been rationalized and defined. It also could not have been done unless customers were used to this kind of standardized "service."

The work that Jack and Sandy do is rooted in having a firm footing in using and being comfortable with computer applications. But it also requires some complex juggling, so that a wide variety of skills and knowledge are compressed into every working hour. Some would say that this represents a break with the rationalization and de-skilling patterns of the 1960s and 1970s. Yet, whether jobs were de-skilled or re-skilled, what was happening was part of the continuing process of redesigning work so that the rationalized pieces could be built into software programs.

Reengineered Jobs and Lives

Corporate reengineering involves a form of work rationalization never imagined by Frederick Taylor and the old scientific management experts in the beginning of the twentieth century. In Taylor's day, there were few machines that could be counted on, and those that were useful were more like individual tools than mechanized systems. Thus Taylor's scientific management studies had to separate and freeze each step of a job so that it could be done faster by people rather than relying on mechanization.[9] By the 1990s, after a long history of applying automation to both factory and office work, managers had a greater range of strategies to call upon. Reengineering and its components became part of a toolbox of techniques that gave top management more control over which jobs could be standardized, which could be combined, which could be integrated through office technology, and which could simply be built into preprogrammed computer applications.

Phrases like "leaner and meaner," "team player," "no pain, no gain," and "work smarter, not harder" made the 1990s downsizing process sound like a team sport. Linking sports metaphors with the often dehumanizing process of reengineering not only heightened the competitive atmosphere, but made it sound like the process was supposed to be fun—once again hiding the difficulties behind an optimistic-sounding set of words, like those of T.Q.M., where it appeared that the emphasis was to be on quality.

In theory, business process reengineering called for organizing the labor process so that costs could be saved by cutting out everything from specific tasks to complete job categories and entire office departments. Sandy's work, with its emphasis on reintegrating tasks through information systems, was part of this process. Jack's work incorporated other reengineering principles, particularly in the way the organization was regrouped into "bands" of workers, instead of a large number of titles and job grades. Today the call center work done by Sandy's operation has been mostly sent out of the country, and the information systems division of the industrial giant Jack worked for has been sold off.

Management experts claim that reengineering is not the same as downsizing or eliminating jobs. Many argue that reengineering should make the organization more competitive and thus create new jobs in other areas. But this, like the technological leap of faith discussed in chapter 1, requires suspending our knowledge of what is actually happening. In the eyes of most corporate "survivors," reorganization and reengineering in the 1990s resulted in fewer jobs and in more work being done with the same number of people—a process that is rapidly spreading to government agencies, educational institutions, and to smaller and newer firms, as we will see in the next two chapters.

Collapsing Job Ladders and Increasing Stress

One of the ways in which reengineering resulted in downsizing was through collapsing job ladders and/or pulling titles out of use, so that workers had to assume more functions and be more "flexible." This type of corporate delayering affects everyone and is still very much in use. It not only changes the labor process (the way work is done), but also affects the labor market, because it results in fewer entry-level positions for people coming into office jobs and fewer opportunities for moving up.

In the years of economic expansion following the Second World War, job ladders were part of what economists call an internal labor market. Job ladders provided a well-marked, bureaucratic career path within a company that offered the chance for promotion and acknowledged that on-the-job training was necessary to move from one rung to the next—from trainee up through a junior level to an associate position, and so on. For people who had made it inside these organizational walls, internal labor markets were both a form of security and a way to think about careers rather than just jobs.

Job ladders had a negative side, however. They worked relatively well for white, college-educated men in organizations where the ladder progressed up through middle management. They were less effective for white college-educated women who—depending on luck (of department or boss)—might make it to the professional ranks but then faced a "glass ceiling" somewhere around lower middle management. They were even less effective for white women who came in through the clerical route, where ladders tended to end with the title of office manager.

For minority men and women, particularly those entering through the mailroom or back-office clerical departments, career ladders were almost nonexistent. The Civil Rights Act of 1963 and the equal opportunity and affirmative action policies of the 1970s helped, but gaining a toehold on the corporate ladder remained extremely difficult. In the 1990s, a clerk-typist, for example, might make it to word–processor, but there the ladder stopped. Similarly, a mailroom clerk might switch to the copy center, but he or she had little chance of moving out of the support area. In other words, for most of the period that job ladders and internal labor markets dominated the organizational landscape, white skin and a college degree appeared to be necessary for movement beyond the lowest organizational rungs. Thirty years after the passage of the Civil Rights Act in the United States, blacks accounted for only 7.5 percent of all managerial and professional occupations.[10]

Unfortunately, job segregation by race and gender was also reflected in the numbers of declining occupations. The effects of the restructuring of work were clearly visible throughout the administrative support area, where a number of jobs simply disappeared. For example, keypunch operators, overwhelmingly minority women, had been phased out by the end of the 1980s. In the 1990s, there was a sustained decline of key administrative support (clerical) job categories. In addition, as companies relied more and more on voice mail and electronic mail, the job of receptionist also began to decline. This is fostered by security concerns: as offices have increasingly turned into locked corridors and closed-off areas, male security guards are more likely than receptionists to be the ones who greet visitors. And telephone operators, a job that once provided a bridge to better work for many women, had begun a significant decline in the early 1990s, leaving only 176,000 operators in 1995.[11]

By the 1990s the pulse of office life was running faster. Sometimes the faster pace could be attributed to computer speed-up, sometimes the fax, sometimes voice mail, but most often it was the way the work had been organized so that fewer people would produce more. Whether this is called efficiency, productivity, or simply speed-up, there are few office occupations where workers do not feel the push to work faster and longer, and to do more.

The quickened pace of office work intensifies physical problems that were first noticed in the 1980s, when computer use was expanding. Growing evidence shows that injuries from repetitive use of the keyboard—commonly called repetitive strain injuries (RSI)—account for at least 60 percent of all workplace injuries. Journalists were among the first to sue their employers because of these problems, particularly tenosynovitis and carpal tunnel syndrome, which come from prolonged rapid use of the keyboard. To avoid these serious problems most experts advise

An example of
multitasking
in the 1990s.
[Jim West]

workers not to sit at the computer for more than two hours at a time, or
for more than twenty hours a week.[12] Yet jobs like customer service representative are designed for people to *sit in one place* and remain at the
keyboard for the working day. And professional and technical workers
usually find themselves sitting at their computers until they get their work
done, which means remaining at the keyboard for longer than recommended periods.

While repetitive strain injuries have made it into the headlines, radiation hazards from computer monitors are not as frequently discussed. Low-
level radiation from monitors is directly linked to severe headaches and to
possible cellular damage, possibly including cancers. Radiation hazards
drop off for people sitting at least an arm's length away from the screen, but
many people lean closer, and at distances of less than two feet electromag-

netic emissions rise rapidly. Electromagnetic radiation from the back of the screen is even higher, which creates problems in poorly designed offices where computers are placed back to back. In addition, the monitors' bright reflective screens can cause a range of serious eye problems.[13]

In ergonomic terms, none of these problems is insurmountable. By the end of the 1980s European countries, for example, set manufacturing standards for monitors and keyboards that lessen these risks. Similarly, many northern European countries have adopted legislation that redesigns jobs so that workers don't have to be in front of computers for longer than recommended time periods. But by the early 1990s, more and more Americans were spending longer and longer hours sitting in front of computers in jobs that had been designed, indeed, reengineered, to ignore these health risks. Today, this is even more so.

Elastic (Broad)bands

As part of the first wave of the reengineering process, job ladders were replaced by different sorts of broad banding, clumping jobs into bands that involve a wide range of presumably interchangeable skills and operational responsibilities, like the bands in Jack's large firm, or Glenda's administrative job with a telecommunications company in chapter 1. Broad banding works something like this: people within a band or category—for example, administrative support—are expected to assume responsibility for a greater number of tasks and for more work. Working in teams, so that any worker can fill in for any other worker, often accompanies broad banding. It is generally assumed that this flexibility increases productivity, and, as anecdotal evidence indicates, most office workers feel they are producing more, as do the companies they work for. A vice president of human resources for a large bank explained it to me this way: "The bottom line is that there are no straight ladders anymore. Employees need to figure out what path they can take and get the skills to do more and prove that they are responsible for doing more. Lateral moves are what they should be looking for."

There is a double standard at work in the creation of teams and broad bands. On the one hand, managers are told to invest in people; on the other hand, they are told to cut out as many people as possible. Business magazines emphasize human potential and building what is called "human capital"—arguing that people can be expected to increase their "worth" through skills and training. A typical example, written in the trendy tone of *Forbes* magazine, states: "Winners [companies] in the Information Age will be evident by their supreme ability to liberate human creativity, create customized products, streamline distribution, get closer to the customer, and cut costs."[14] Like so much we hear, this reiterates the key phrases that gurus of reengineering use in their effort to sugarcoat the often bitter pill of reengineered jobs.

Job bands may, in theory, "liberate" creativity by giving people room to do more and different tasks (if this is in fact a form of liberation), but their bottom-line purpose is to cut costs. And cutting costs generally limits the number of jobs and therefore the opportunities for promotion. And when occupational bands are used in conjunction with longer periods between salary reviews and coupled with the use of temps who work side by side with full-time employees, they are reminders to full-time employees that they may be only one step away from temporary or jobless status.

Networked!

Networks became as central to the first half of the 1990s as personal computers were to the 1980s. By 1994, 87 percent of large firms and 32 percent of smaller companies had some form of local area network (LAN).[15] And increasing number of organizations also installed wide area networks (WANs), which linked computers in different departments, buildings, and cities. During this time the Internet, a previously academic and scientific network, was beginning to be opened for commercial processes.

Networks were a technical development waiting to happen. In the 1980s, we saw how users, managers, and systems analysts were frustrated by the lack of compatible software and what technicians call standard protocols, which allow information sent from one computer—via modem or through a local network—to be received on another computer. By the mid-1990s, agreements between hardware and software companies, along with industry-wide standards, smoothed out the majority of preexisting hardware and software compatibility problems. These were not, in any case, so much technical problems as situations that required companies and the government to sit down and hammer out standards they could all adhere to. The standards then gave companies room to carve out their market niches, as the history of the Internet clearly shows.

Setting such network standards fit in well with plans to remove middle managers and incorporate the information and reports they had once generated directly into databases that could be brought up on different computer screens, whenever and whereever they were needed. Network standards also fit in with reengineering plans that called for abolishing lower-level tasks like data entry and repackaging them (at least temporarily) into integrated jobs—like Sandy's job at a bank's call center.

Networks also supported organizations that wanted to divide their labor force geographically and get more output from the same number of workers—or, where possible, fewer workers. This was still another aspect of business process reengineering: moving people, offices, and functions around in an attempt to lower real estate costs as well labor costs. In 1994, a chief technology officer for a large bank explained how his bank's network was increasing productivity by decreasing the number of so-called data-processing centers in the United States from 100 to two—one in New York and one in London. The remaining centers operated with a fraction of the former workforce, and when one center has too much processing, the overflow was switched across the Atlantic.[16] Investment in more reliable and standardized hardware and software, along with access to leased network lines, made it possible for management to cut payrolls and provided the flexibility to keep them cut, as discussed in the next chapter.[17] Surprisingly, with hindsight we can now see that the changes in white-collar work practices in the first half of the 1990s were made, for the most part, without the infrastructure of the Internet.

6. The Late 1990s: Enter the Internet

Most important, perhaps, this new medium came along at a time when corporate managers were questioning the meager benefits delivered by two decades of lavish investment in IT infrastructure.

—Rose, *No-Collar,* 2002[1]

Most accounts of Internet history start with something like "with the advent of the Internet," making it seem like technology, with all its multiple layers, such as hardware, software, infrastructure, and standards, burst on the scene in full form. Still other accounts tell of a history of heroes and hackers who seemingly single-handedly "invented" parts of the Internet. What follows here, however, is a more complex story: one told from the perspective of how individuals, organizations, universities, governments, consumers, and indeed social and political cultures along with economic demands, formed the basis of what we know and use as Internet technology.

Two notable birthdays mark the Internet's coming of age. The first, in 1990, connotes the coming together of the pieces we call World Wide Web through programs that could share both textual and graphic information. And the second, in 1995, is marked by the beginning of widespread use of the browser called Netscape, an interface program that enabled users to visually link text and graphics.

According to economists and business leaders the Internet was to be the linchpin of a new economy, an economy so strong that it could withstand business cycles. Indeed, many claimed that the introduction of the Internet was the cutting edge of a second Industrial Revolution. *Fortune* magazine, always ready to pronounce a new era, claimed in 1998, for example, that "the [computer] chip has already transformed our lives at least as pervasively as the internal-combustion engine or the electric motor."[2] As Doug Henwood stated in the opening of his book *After the New Economy,* "Between 1996 and 2001, you could hardly have opened a newspaper or turned on a TV without hearing about the wondrous new economy."[3] But alas, the new economy with its promised millions of knowledge industry jobs and recession-proof economy was to have a puzzling and short-lived history. By 2000 and 2001, Internet company stock prices had plunged, and newly created dot-com jobs were rapidly disappearing as were IT jobs in other organizations. We will return to this in the next chapter.

In 2000, Alan Greenspan, chairman of the Federal Reserve Board and chief architect of the new economy's monetary policy, argued that "it is the proliferation of information technology throughout the economy that makes the current period appear so *different* [italics added] from preceding decades." But his meaning of a different type of economy is explained more fully in the rest of a speech he gave, entitled "Structural Change in the New Economy":

> One result of the more-rapid pace of IT innovation has been a visible acceleration of the process that noted economist Joseph Schumpeter many years ago termed "creative destruction"—the continuous shift in which emerging technologies push out the old. He goes on to add that IT enables businesses to "reduce unnecessary inventory and dispense with labor and capital redundancies."[4]

In the lives of working people this process of creative destruction is one where the widespread distribution of Internet connections has meant exciting new sources of information and entertainment (although as many would argue not necessarily creative sources), but it has brought with it as well an intensification of unstable labor market and labor process conditions that had begun to be visible before. As we saw in the last chapter, the first half of the 1990s was marked by corporate downsizing that dumped large swatches of middle-income white-collar workers outside of corporate walls and an acceleration of contracting out former employees to subcontracting firms. The contracting out process, known as outsourcing, was speeded up in the second half of the decade by both corporate efforts to raise stock prices through lowering labor costs and through the use of distributed technologies—chiefly connected through Internet expansion.

The first complete report of workplace computer and Internet use was done by the U.S. Bureau of Labor Statistics in a 2001 survey. The report estimated that 72 million people used computers at work, and in white-collar occupations more than 79 percent of managerial and professional workers used computers, with 65.8 percent using the Internet.[5] While no reliable baseline data exists to mark the way that Internet use had grown, these percentages, indicate that from the first Internet browser use in the early 1990s, more than 75 percent of professional workers were online by 2001. A remarkable change, particularly if one takes *Business Week* reports into account, for, as one analyst put it, "as recently as 1998, surveys showed that most CEOs didn't know how to open their own e-mail, much less make wise technology decisions."[6]

In analyzing how all of these changes appeared to come about so quickly I will first explore a brief history of the various Internet technologies that took root during this period. I will then discuss the way the work and jobs have been divided into smaller and different parcels. The next chapter will highlight how the job fragments were outsourced to other companies and other countries.

Through the Interface

What we call the Internet, or simply the Net, is a series of different technologies, standards, and conventions intertwined with an array of computer manufacturers, software development firms, telecommunications companies, and government as well as international agencies. All of it is held together by people—those who use it, for work, play, information, entertainment—and those who work in one of the companies or agencies that create, code, and support it. The Internet is no one thing or one type of technology, but rather a series of layers. What many techies think of as the bottom layer is made up of switching circuits that send packets of data from one node or computer to another. A basic building block of the Internet was the idea that groups of data could be bundled together into packets and distributed around it through computer gateways, depending on which parts of the Net were available at any given time. What used to be known simply as *data* processing was transformed into information technology—the IT field—as computers and telecommunications were joined to rapidly spread increasingly ubiquitous information around the world.

Like other parts of computer systems, the packets are carried along not just by the signals and circuits, but also by the software that instructs the computers about what to do with the packets of data. This level of software is called the operating system software, and it works hand-in-glove with the telecommunications software that handles when and where packets of information should get off the network and downloaded into a particular computer at a given address. On top of that layer are the applications programs that link databases with different information sources, as well as enable online purchasing and electronic interchange of funds. As users, we generally see only the top levels of software; the interface that interacts between the operating system and what we see on our screens and application programs like Word. Interface software includes the contested terrain of browsers and search engines that corporations are battling for control.

The Internet evolved over time, as people in a variety of occupations and places around the world worked to shake the bugs out of each type of hardware and each development in software. It also took time because there were many people and companies involved; each building on work done by others before them. The following gives an overview of some of the social and political history that is part of these layers.

Building the Base

The Internet, as a physical network, is formed from nodes or computers that are connected in a decentralized structure. Just as our own human networks may be made up of people we see regularly and those we only have occasional contact with, each node or computer in a network is independent and can "communicate" with any other node known to it, at any time. In 1969 the U.S. Defense Department, considered one of the most centralized organizations, ironically adapted this concept of *decentralized* technical networking when it, together with a group of research universities, formed ARPANET (Advanced Research Projects Agency Network).[7]

This odd association of the rigid and bureaucratic structure of the military, and its reliance on decentralized, loosely associated university network nodes, needs to be viewed through the context of the cold war. In 1957 the Russians launched Sputnik, bringing about a heated-up arms race between the United States and the Soviet Union. In this cold war climate, the following year the U.S. Defense Department put research universities together with a newly established Advanced Research Projects Agency to fund joint science and technology projects. Given the military arms race of the 1950s and 1960s ARPANET was not such a strange entity, because the U.S. military put a premium on building a computer and communications network that could survive a nuclear attack. Thus a decentralized computer network was the foundation of ARPANET's design.

Standards and protocols were needed in order to pull together the loose decentralized computer connections so that data could be more easily shunted between the connected nodes. To better understand the need for technical protocols we can again turn to the social arena where protocols are used for communicating diplomatically. In 1973 a network of networks was established built on the concept that each node, or computer connection, would be using a Transmission Control Protocol (TCP) as well as an Inter-network Protocol (IP). While the ARPANET did not necessarily rely on these standards, the Defense Department solidified all of its communications using them, and today these TCP/IPs are in use worldwide. By 1990 the ARPANET had been decommissioned but the inter-net—or international collection of decentralized computer nodes—was in place, sending, receiving, and exchanging billions of characters of data hourly through standardized protocols.

A Tangled Web

Once the inter-network had computer nodes, protocols, and software in place, more people began to use it, and economic and political problems obviously emerged. Contrary to what many people think, there wasn't any one type of hardware or software component that was best; rather, use of the Net gave rise to a lot of issues requiring agreements between organizations and governments. Issues to be ironed out included which manufacturers' standards should be used, which country's protocols were to dominate, and whether governments or commercial interests should have the primary say over the emerging international network. As did the fundamental question of how addresses for each computer on the *inter*national *net*work of networks would be assigned so that messages could be sent to, and received in, the right places.

The United States and Europe, the dominant regions in building the Internet, presented two markedly different perspectives on how these questions should be resolved. In 1976, the International Telecommunications Union in Europe endorsed a protocol that was not compatible with TCP/IP. This standard, known as x.25, was favored by the large Post and Telecommunications bureaus (PTTs) in Europe. And the PTTs were set to act as public telecommunications agencies. Building on this experience, by the early 1980s France had set up MINITEL, an extensive network of home computer–like terminals where people could send and receive messages.

In the United States meanwhile, computer and software companies along with universities moved in the opposite direction, steering Internet standards and governance away from governmental mandates. Interestingly, ARPANET, a government-sponsored project, was increasingly being used in the private sector by universities and corporations. Since ARPANET's protocols allowed for differing and layered standards, this approach turned out to be more inclusive and began to win out over the European model of government standards.

Some Internet histories, particularly those told through the voices of hackers as freedom-loving individuals, claim that the adoption of TCP/IP was a bottom-up grassroots approach to building the Internet rather than a centralized government-imposed model.[8] In part this is so, as the open architecture of the Internet allows for independent nodes to be connected to each other through a single protocol that evolved out of use. But this does not mean that the Internet is necessarily a grassroots instrument of change. Rather the real struggles over control of parts of the net—the technical hardware and software layers and the information transmitted—are being fought out among corporate giants around the world.

The establishment of a standard and mechanism for assigning computer addresses followed a similar debate along the lines of whether or not to centralize the allocation of addresses and which types of organizations should be responsible for doing so. Early on, as part of the centralized approach, the International Telecommunications Union set up a committee to assign network addresses to each country. But embedded in this approach was the 1970s assumption that computer addresses would be assigned only to large mainframe computers and that there wouldn't be many of these in each country. Again, and not surprisingly, the opposite approach was undertaken in the United States where the management for assigning Internet domain names worldwide (which link to unique addresses), was given to a nonprofit, private U.S. organization, the Internet Corporation for Assigned Names and Numbers (ICAAN). ICAAN has become, de facto, the world's Internet governance organization, but its control over the Internet is now being challenged in the United Nations by developing nations as Internet use has spread to Africa, South America, and Asia.[9]

While the discussions over standards were going on, the major corporate players were also beginning to fight it out over where Internet profits would come from and who would dominate which newly emerging market. In the 1980s computer hardware manufacturers, including companies making computer chips, locked horns in corporate battles over which company's standards would dominate the market for computers. IBM's dominance in the hardware industry came as a surprise to firms like Apple that had appeared as the early leaders. By the end of the 1990s IBM had gained a monopoly position in the market for PCs.

Demonstrating a way that the new economy might not be very new, Microsoft repeated IBM's ploy by grabbing a monopoly in the software industry in the 1990s. By installing their own browser, Internet Explorer, on all Windows operating systems, they ripped the lead away from Netscape's Navigator by 1997 and seized almost total control of this key piece of software by 1998. Despite a number of antitrust cases and settlement agreements against Microsoft, and despite the fact that Netscape's Navigator and its innovative updates were credited with ushering in widespread use of the

World Wide Web, Microsoft used its monopoly position with the Windows operating system to stake their 90 percent control over yet another world-wide monopoly.[10] In the basics of capitalism, monopolistic control of markets is the rule, rather than the exception.[11]

As it became clear that information technology was also about entertainment and networks, corporate battles in the later part of the 1990s and the early new century shifted to the companies that were to control the transmission of information. This placed multinational telecommunication firms in the forefront of the competition as traditional telephone companies vied with each other to compete with media giants and entertainment firms. These battles are still being fought as huge multinationals, like Viacom and TimeWarner/AOL, merge and buy out other firms.[12]

Users, Uses, Work and Play

Manuel Castells, social scientist and author of the *Internet Galaxy* and other widely read books on the history and implications of the Internet, reminds us how the movers and shakers behind many so-called technological breakthroughs, are really the people who use the technology:

> It is a proven lesson from the history of technology that users are key producers of the technology, by adapting it to their uses and values, and ultimately transforming the technology itself.[13]

Throughout the 1990s the search was on in the software industry for "killer apps"—software applications that people would choose over anything else. One of the first drivers of the Internet was e-mail, an application that few predicted would amount to much. Indeed critics claimed that people would always prefer to talk on the phone, rather than write. An e-mail program called Eudora (freely available from 1988 until it was bought by Qualcomm in 1994) was a huge hit with the millions of people who were beginning to sign up with small Internet Service Provider (ISP) companies in order to get online from home. Businesses were slow to catch on to the advantages of e-mail and many corporate IT departments had to scramble to add e-mail to their company networks in the mid-1990s.[14]

Another surprising development was widespread use of online communities. Groundwork for online communities had been set in the 1980s as earlier home-based computer users (not necessarily computer specialists) established what came to be called virtual communities. Some online communities, like for example, the WELL, started in the San Francisco area in 1985, hosted discussion groups, while others were made up of people playing multiple-user games (including MUDs or Multi-User Dungeons), mailing lists, online conferences, as well as bulletin board systems (BBS) for community announcements.[15] By the time that the Internet had been commercialized in the mid-1990s, corporate strategic management had begun to borrow pages from home user practice, introducing company bulletin boards, mailing lists, and online conferences into workplace IT systems.

The Rise and Fall of IT Jobs

To be sure, the number of IT jobs in the United States increased markedly at the end of the twentieth century. According to the Bureau of Labor Statistics, the number of computer programmers grew from 553,000 in 1995 to 699,000 in 2000, and the number of computer systems analysts jumped significantly from 933,000 to 1,787,000 in the same period.[16] While these more traditional and higher salaried computer occupations were growing, IT support—including jobs like database administrator, help desk technician, webmaster, and IT specialists—were gaining even faster, although the Bureau of Labor Statistics was not geared up to keep track of them. Even more significant was the fact that IT jobs were no longer just in IT industries but had spread out throughout all organizations—including health care, schools, arts institutions, and sports—as Internet and computer applications became ubiquitous. Reliable estimates about job growth in IT-related areas are difficult to find since neither the government nor independent agencies kept track of the meteoric rise of new IT jobs and work titles. The Commerce Department reported that IT occupations totaled 5.4 million at their high point in 2000, although this appears to include computer manufacturing jobs, which were the first to be outsourced abroad.[17] According to the Computer Technology Industry Association, there were approximately 2.6 million service and support jobs in Information

Technology with 10 percent of these remaining unfilled by 1999 because of a labor shortage.[18]

The most heralded work in the later half of the 1990s was that of the so-called no-collar, new media workers—the programmers, commercial artists, and young businesspeople who developed websites and multimedia projects. These emerging and merged occupations grew out of older job categories, and grew with such a frenzy that by the turn of the century, jobs, companies, and indeed the whole industry had all but almost disappeared in what came to be known as the bust of the dot-com bubble. Here is an account of this remarkable microcosm of the growth and collapse of job titles, jobs, and the reorganization of work, as told through the eyes of two people who's lives and work changed during this period.

When I first interviewed Tim in 1997 he was a part of a "financial" group—an inter-occupational cluster of people working on developing websites and intranets (internal information nets) for firms in the financial services sector.

> *Tim's corner of the light-filled loft office is a cozy collection of pieces of old computers, a skateboard, a collage of odd photographs, and a tower of CDs for his headphones.*

> *"I love coding," he says as he heads off into the café corner of the loft so that we could continue our discussion without interrupting the others in his work cluster. "See, I get to use what I know and get to learn new stuff all the time; it's almost like creating something out of nothing. And I get paid real well, and then there is always the stock options."*

Two years later his group had been reorganized and the desks and work surfaces scattered into a new pattern, where Tim focused only on website interfaces for existing customer databases. The company had also acquired two smaller advertising firms and had begun to branch out into more general "new media" consulting.

> *"Lots of the people coming from advertising and the commercial world are doing their own Web development now using applications that it doesn't take a programmer to know. But my end of the work is still really important because I am the guy that ties it all together with my code."*

At that time Tim worked with information and systems architects—budding new industry titles—who were the people who decided what the interface screens would look like and how they would fit in with the existing or legacy company databases. His focus was on writing the small but critically important bits of computer code that would make the old and new pieces fit together.

The shuffle of desks, work spaces, work groups, job titles, and work was to change for Tim again as the company was bought by a larger consulting firm. The newer organization of over 150 people had a formal personnel system of job titles and pay scales and had begun to implement standard "practices" in order to ensure that clients got their Web "products" by the deadlines they had contracted for. His company withstood the shock waves of the dot-com stock market crash in 2000, but it did so as an international consulting company, one that was more focused on marketing and business databases than on clever, "artsy" website design. Tim was lucky and left before the stock market bubble burst, and decided to go to graduate school.

> *"It wasn't like it was a really calculated decision," he explained. "Rather, I just couldn't stand the boredom of coding the same stuff all the time and working those long hours. I figured that grad school couldn't be any worse."*

David, on the other hand, was hired in 1997 as a software test engineer by a large, very well-known software firm. The company was organized around project teams that worked on each of its software products (word processing, spreadsheets, etc.). These teams, small and inter-occupational, were composed of people who specialized in specific parts of each product. David was the tester who worked on checking if each feature change in a database program connected with the Web interface.

> *"At first I loved the office environment," he said, "because there were no cubicles and the people were really incredible." But within a few years he found that he "really didn't like testing" because "it really is too negative a job and people don't want to hear about what doesn't work."*

The software giant David worked for, in an effort to keep up with the emerging Silicon Alley and Silicon Valley smaller firms, brought in comedians to entertain at corporate meetings and arranged pizza deliveries for the sometimes 75-hour workweeks when teams were working to get software products shipped. David was "let go" in 2003 as part of the corporation's ongoing downsizing.

> *"By the time I left the work was so well documented that anyone could do the job. The pressure was always on to 'get your bug count up' [fix problems or "bugs" in the software], which meant that management was looking at numbers, and not at what the bugs were about."[19]*

The changes David experienced had been foreshadowed by Braverman's classic study of labor process changes in the industrial era. Braverman's *Labor and Monopoly Capitalism* detailed the de-skilling or downgrading of skills among factory workers.[20] As we saw in earlier chapters, a similar kind of sharp specialization and streamlining of work also happened to other white-collar workers in the '60s and '70s. This newer version of rationalization and specialization of work, however, was happening faster within the hothouse environment of corporate reorganization, downsizing, mergers and acquisitions, and the forerunner of outsourcing—contracting out.

Dot-Bust

In the late 1990s, when many small Internet and new media firms were growing and being bought out by larger firms, the industry was a major cornerstone in the then booming stock market. Financial analysts and others representing financial firms rapidly put together proposals for initial public offerings (IPOs) to create and sell shares in the new firms in what the analysts promised would be the new economy. Workers in these new hybrid companies—artists and designers from advertising and entertainment, M.B.A.s and marketing experts in business consulting, information technology specialists—were often offered the chance and the excitement of buying the stock offerings. For most workers the stock options became what seemed like a dream—far more wealth than their salaries or even bonuses could have ever provided.

Stories in the popular press played into the much-heralded hype about the dot-com millionaires and their visions and pronouncements about a new economy where each employee would be an owner. The new employ-ee-owner millionaires came to symbolize the possibilities of a new postin-dustrial economy in the same way that stories of Horatio Alger, a fictional rags-to-riches character, did in the industrial period of the late nineteenth century. For young people entering into these firms the lure of individual wealth, represented by shares in stock, held out the promise of more inter-esting jobs and a better work life than the corporate career-ladder paths of their parents' generation.

By the spring of 2000, however, the so-called dot-com bubble had burst in the stock market, and by most accounts several hundred thousand peo-ple were fired from Silicon Valley (Northern California), Silicon Alley (New York City), and other Internet-intensive areas. It is estimated that more than a million others in a wide range of older industries like finance, insur-ance, and legal sectors were also laid off in the United States.[21]

In some ways the crash of the stock prices for Internet-related firms was not remarkable. By standard capitalist accounting practices, companies like Amazon.com, then the first major online retailer, had no reported earnings. In theory, new economy firms were supposed to create new forms of wealth and financial capital through digital exchanges—a sort of virtual capital-ism. In practice, however, capitalism expands through the growth of capi-tal; simply put, money makes more money. The Internet-related firms, while promising riches, were not actually creating or distributing more money into the economy, although they followed the old economic pattern where larger firms kept on buying out smaller firms.

In addition to the effect of Internet-related companies on the larger economy, these firms were also supposed to be different in their work prac-tices and working conditions. Again, in theory, workers who were owners (at least of stock certificates) were to have more of a say over what they did and to have a chance to acquire new skills and use them in more creative ways. Unlike older more bureaucratic or hierarchical management models, the new economy was to be characterized by flattened channels of commu-nication between workers and their managers. Working hours, dress codes, and office walls as well as office furniture were to reflect a more flexible working culture. To be sure, these characteristics were in place for hundreds of thousands of workers who did manage to get in on the ground floor of Internet-related companies.[22]

According to Bill Gates in his best-selling book *The Road Ahead,* the Internet and related technologies were supposed to usher in an era of "friction-free capitalism."[23] Gates, along with many in the business press, proclaimed that perfect control over information—the new hot commodity—would lead to better, more efficient markets. Presumably, more efficient markets were to be ones with more competition. But for firms like Microsoft its traditional monopoly position in the software industry gave it the lead to take perfect control and record-breaking profits in the browser market. Other corporations like Viacom maneuvered themselves into higher profits by buying out other firms that tried to compete with them in telecommunications and entertainment. Indeed, Gates spelled this out himself, in explaining how growing market concentrations work: "This is why cable companies, regional telephone companies, and consumer-electronics manufacturers are rushing to work with Hollywood studios, television and cable broadcasters, and other content businesses."[24]

This pattern of rapid monopoly control over key markets was not a result of the new information technologies and the Internet, but rather part and parcel of capitalism-as-usual. The introduction and widespread use of the telegraph in the nineteenth century, the telephone and radio in the early twentieth century, and television in midcentury followed the same path. In the article "Virtual Capitalism: The Political Economy of the Information Highway," the authors argue that

> history has shown that every technological revolution in communications—no matter what its potential for democratization has been—has lent itself to the growth of new monopolies of information when inscribed within existing systems of social and economic power.[25]

The "existing systems of social and economic power" in the 1990s had begun to take on a strong current of what was known as "market liberalization"—worldwide strategies meant to keep governments away from regulating markets, leaving companies freer to engage in whatever business practices and takeovers they so chose.

While overall economic patterns of the 1990s appeared as a speeded-up version of capitalism-as-usual, a new set of work relations had emerged out of the economic shake-ups of the late 1990s and early twenty-first century. These new work relations do not appear to reflect the gloss that was placed on them in the mid-1990s—worker-owners with many jobs to choose from and flexible working conditions. Rather they show a major shift in employment relations for people entering the labor market as well as for experienced workers. The shifts are apparent in the way workers—all workers from factory floors to freelance professionals—are expected to be more flexible in terms of their job expectations, salary, contractual arrangement, time spent doing work, and skills. The next chapter details how these different work relations have changed people's expectations about jobs and where and when work is done.

7. The Office of the Future is Everywhere

At first the work was mostly limited to call centers—phone American Express with a query about a corporate card bill, and there's a good chance you'll be talking to Delhi. But in the past two or three years companies have turned to India and the Philippines for much more sophisticated tasks: financial analysis, software design, tax preparation, and even the creation of PowerPoint presentations.

—*Fortune*, June 2003[1]

The much-heralded new economy of the 1990s, with its supposed recession-proof shock absorbers built on productivity generated by technology, did not materialize in the twenty-first century. In 2002, the Bureau of Labor Statistics reported that 32.1 million jobs in the United States had been lost, many of them in occupations requiring skill and higher education. The same statistics reported that 31.7 million jobs had been "created," but as most people know, these newer jobs include part-time and low-wage sales jobs like those at the super-discount chain Wal-Mart.[2] Indeed the economic lesson of the 1990s was not about the end of the business cycle in one country, but rather about the distribution of economic effects around the globe as employers sought out cheaper labor sources in country after country. Explaining the basics of capitalist labor economics and its built-in drive to lower *all* wages, *Business Week* put it this way:

Indeed, trade theory suggests that the impact ultimately could be larger for high-skilled workers than it has been for the lesser-educated. As the world increasingly begins to look like one big labor pool, market forces should tend to move wages everywhere toward the same level for similar work, all else being equal.

The author, Aaron Bernstein, then goes on to explain how wages worldwide can race to the bottom: "After all," he says, "a software programmer with sufficient smarts and education needs only an office, a computer, and plenty of caffeine to do a good job. So if an Indian programmer can produce as much high-quality code as an American one, wage equalization for programmers may occur at a faster pace than it has for apparel workers."[3]

To economists, then, the outsourcing of high-end jobs—computer programming, accounting, engineering and architectural planning—to countries with lower wages should have been expected, although the business press seemed at first to be surprised by it. In the 1990s, the pundits in the press had continually reported management's message of the increasing need for more knowledge workers. But now it was becoming clear that the combination of embedding routine parts of jobs into computer software and databases, coupled with the decreasing costs of information infrastructure, opened the doors for an exodus of jobs from first world countries like the United States and Britain to former colonial and Soviet bloc countries where workers are educated, disciplined, and hungry for this kind of work.

But the shock value of the media recognizing that high-tech and high-skill jobs could be exported was but one part of the story about the changing nature of work. The other parts had been seen on a smaller scale throughout the 1990s, namely, the increasing part-time and contingent nature of the jobs that stayed in this country; the extended reliance on defining work in terms of projects or products instead of specific hours worked; enhanced expectations that consumers would do their own work, on the Web or on the phone; and the tremendous reduction in the cost of computer hardware, software, and networks. All of which came together to create what seemed to be a vortex that sucked jobs out of the country and made the remaining ones more stressful and more full of risks. For remaining workers these risks included not knowing where the next job or project would come from, as well as the very down-to-earth risk of getting sick and not having medical insurance or paid sick leave.

In an article entitled "Is Your Job Next?" *Business Week* explained the steps to offshore work:

It's globalization's next wave—and one of the biggest trends reshaping the global economy. The first wave started two decades ago with the exodus of jobs making shoes, cheap electronics, and toys to developing countries. After that, simple service work, like processing credit-card receipts, and mind-numbing digital toil, like writing software code, began fleeing high-cost countries. For corporations that had previously outsourced jobs like product design, technical support, and employee benefits to subcontractors in their home country, the step for corporations in the U.S., France, Germany and Scandinavia was shifting jobs to overseas subcontracting firms. ...Now, all kinds of knowledge work can be done almost anywhere.[4]

All these changes are part of a familiar economic pattern of shifting financial risk from large organizations to smaller ones, and from higher management to the individual worker. In the 1980s, managers talked of needing "just-in-time" products in order to compete in the global market. By the late 1990s, in addition to flexible product inventories, employees too have become a just-in-time variable. Originally "just in time" meant that parts and products would be produced, as they were needed, thus reducing the expense of keeping inventories. In the world of office work, just-in-time workers are those drawn from the contingent workforce, where companies hire them only during peak periods. This has many advantages for the firm but comparatively few for the worker, except for those self-employed consultants in professional areas, many of whom say that they prefer this arrangement.[5]

Some of the strategies in earlier waves of reorganization had been borrowed (somewhat loosely) from Japanese management strategies, which caught the interest of U.S. managers in the 1980s. For instance, autoworkers in Japan assembled cars, but the majority of parts were made by smaller subcontracting firms whose "peripheral" workers could be called in as needed. In the United States as in Japan this led to a two-tiered workforce: core employees with the "parent" firm and peripheral workers in the subcontracting firms, each with different pay scales and job titles. Core workers are in effect more permanent employees who are more likely to have health benefits, sick leave, and pensions. Peripheral workers, on the other hand, are part of what economists call the secondary labor market, with their job security and wages dependent on the sales of the subcontractor's product, as well as on the number of other peripheral workers competing for their jobs. It had been a successful system for producing low-priced cars, but it is a brutal way to treat workers in the labor market.[6]

By now it is clear that the creation of a "just-in-time" production process has spread further and been applied throughout the white-collar sector, not only in the United States and Japan, but throughout the world. Now parent companies, including large firms in India, squeeze competitive prices out of subcontracting firms, who in turn squeeze lower-priced contracts out of the large reserve labor pool of individual freelancers and self-employed workers, many of whom are willing to take whatever comes along to pay the bills.

Knowledge Industry?

The center of the knowledge industry—the university—is one of the most visible places to see how work and the places it is done in have changed.[7] According to the American Association of University Professors (AAUP) three out of five positions in universities in the United States are taught by full-time and part-time contingent, or non-tenure track, faculty. Only one-fourth of these contingent instructors have appointments of more than two semesters.[8] This is a hefty temporary workforce, charged with preparing the next generation of educated workers.

Traditionally the majority of adjuncts had been graduate students, for whom teaching part-time was a kind of apprenticeship for working their way through their doctoral studies. Increasingly, however, universities have relied on hiring more part-timers and non-tenured faculty to lower labor costs and increase the number of sections taught and thus raise university income. This push to cut costs and increase revenue at universities, linked to the need for income by out-of-work and part-time professionals, has resulted in a growing army of freelance academics. Marilyn, a sociology adjunct instructor, teaching at two different colleges, tells how scattered and time-intensive this work is:

"This is my office," she says, lifting the lid on the trunk of her car. "And I'm lucky to have it. Many people I know commute by bus or train and they have to lug around this much stuff." For Marilyn, the "stuff" she points to is barely contained in two cardboard boxes; one largely made up of the tools of her trade—her books, a laptop computer, chalk, pens and paper, some lecture and class notes and some notebooks; the other holds student papers to grade.

"I'm teaching three courses this semester at two different colleges. One course has forty-five students, but the other two are just under thirty. You do the math," she says, pointing at the pile of student papers. "With an average of thirty students in a class and two written exams and two research/project papers per course, that's 120 written papers per course or 360 for the semester. Multiply that times the number of pages per paper, and it's out of control; I'm reading every morning before class and late into the evenings, and of course most of the weekend."

Marilyn had hoped to be in a tenure-track job by now, but has admittedly slowed down on her work toward her doctorate because the academic job market is so weak and because her adjunct work keeps her from her research. If she works for a whole year her pay for three courses a semester (the equivalent of a full-time job) is under $25,000 a year.

Tenured or more permanent jobs inside of university walls have also changed. Everyone I interviewed spoke of increasing workload, which ranged from more students per semester to more papers to grade, to more time spent on a computer doing administrative work, and to more e-mail to answer. The last is a relatively new phenomenon in the practice of teaching and learning. But as both faculty and students have become more used to being online, e-mail and course websites have become a common extension of the educational environment. The U.S. Department of Education reported that in 2001—the first wave of online courses—there were almost 3 million students enrolled in for-credit online courses, up from 1.3 million in 1997.[9]

At another college, Anita, a full-time, tenured associate professor invited me into her office to show me her new course site. Five years earlier, in an attempt "to enable faculty to be comfortable with computers" the college had given each faculty member a computer, along with an e-mail account and

A home office. [Jim West]

access to the Internet. While the college invested part of a new student technology fee for faculty and student computers, there were no funds allocated for additional office space or computer furniture. I had to stand in the doorway of Anita's office to peer over her shoulder at the computer monitor that was plunked on top of her desk, well above her eye level. She was using a packaged computer application called Blackboard, to put together supplemental materials for the students in one of her classroom-based courses.

> *"I was offered the chance to do an online course, but I didn't want to do it until I tried it out. So this course," she says as she points to a website for an Introduction to Computing course, "is one that I was already teaching, and I just thought that I would add a website with course materials and a Discussion Board. Ha. It's a great idea, and the students seem to love it and I love it, but boy is it more work. They think I'm available 24/7: 'Professor, I have one more question.' they write, and I'm an idiot, because I am reading it at 2 A.M. I'm going to have to learn how to be more disciplined with my time."*

Many faculty, like other professional workers, see the extension of their working day as their problem—one they have to work out by managing their time more carefully. But the reality of the situation is that the time squeeze on people in work and home settings is a societal issue. While it is easy to "blame it on the Internet" the rising human cost of overwork and the blurred boundaries between home, commuting, work, study, shopping, ordering, and other activities can't simply be placed at the door of the Internet as if it were an outside revolutionizing force.

We experience all sorts of change in our daily lives in two contradictory ways. On the one hand we experience some things like changes in work practice as inching along at an almost incremental pace. On the other hand we see some change like that involving technology, as charging at us with incredible speed. Much of our perception of change is shaped by what we read and hear and are taught to look for. Technological change, we are told, is revolutionary, and its history is told in galloping episodes like the introduction of the printing press, the steam engine, and the computer, each leading to massive changes in society. Work and home life, we are led to believe, is fairly constant over time, with expectations changing every generation or so, through economic conditions like the Great Depression of the 1930s, or bottom-up social change like the struggle for civil and economic rights for Black Americans and women in the 1960s and 1970s.[10] Yet social and organizational change is often as rapid and visible as the technical gadgets we see around us.

Both perceptions feel valid at different points in time, but the narrative we are told about the revolutionary nature of technology dominates our view of experience.[11] Anita, for example, felt that being online made the students perceive that she was available around the clock. And indeed e-mail and websites have this potential. But her college had invested in computers and software and had hired many computer support personnel to lay the foundation long before she began to extend her course on-line. Her decision to extend her course—a change in work practice—was the impetus that led her to experience the overload. The teaching work practice had been undergoing change for a number of years as universities, taking a page from the corporate world, learned to rely more heavily on quantitative measurements for faculty productivity.

In the late 1990s universities embraced online education as a way of reaching more students and cutting costs. As corporations had rushed to usher in a new era of "virtual offices" in the 1990s, so had universities been quick to predict a future of "distance learning" and enhanced university earnings without the brick-and-mortar expense of expanding campuses. Both the virtual office and the online university didn't come along with the revolutionary speed they were supposed to. Indeed, by 2001–02 major universities, like Columbia and New York University, found that the specialized, online companies they had announced with fanfare were not financially viable.[12] But the following year other large universities were back to expanding their online course offerings, this time using the corporate model of expanding to new markets through buying and merging with universities in other countries. An example of this occurred in 2003, when the New School University, a leader in adult education, formed a partnership with the Open University in England, the world's largest distance education system.[13]

Union organizing in higher education has been picking up steam, particularly among part-time and graduate student workers. The United Auto Workers (called the "United Academic Workers" in an article in the *Chronicle of Higher Education*) jumped into the organizing stream along with the American Federation of Teachers (AFT) and the National Educational Association (NEA) in organizing part-time university employees —one of the fastest-growing segments of labor organizing in the early twenty-first century.[14]

University employees, like medical doctors, are finding their decision making constrained by bureaucratic levels of corporate managers and vice presidents. Ironically, as corporate managers now claim that the older hierarchical corporate structure is inefficient, this model is being propagated among formerly independent professionals in health care and higher education. There is little new in this pattern, for increased levels of management have been added to control those workers thought to be too independent— from craftsman in the early industrial period to bookkeepers and accountants in the early white collar post–Second World War period. Once managerial control over the workers and the work process is achieved, upper management releases some hierarchical reins, as professionals then internalize the demands and don't need to be reminded of the rules on a routine basis.[15]

Not in One Place

In the twenty-first century, large international corporations continued to fire midlevel managerial, professional, and administrative workers, as they had begun to do in the downsizing craze of the early 1990s. Bank employees, the cornerstone of the financial service sector, were particularly affected as broad-stroke organizational changes like continued mergers, closed branch offices, and enhanced reliance on computer and Web-based banking were pushed on the workforce in waves. This meant massive changes for those still employed in banking. Among the interviews I conducted in an international megabank, I spoke with Julia, an officer in charge of arranging the technical and physical support for employee moves within the company. After fifteen minutes spent passing security at the New York office, Julia greeted me at the electronic card entry point to her floor. Once past the heavy glass doors we were in a narrow interior corridor and surrounded by chairs, desks, tables, cables, and stacks of computer equipment. Edging our way past the jumble she ushered me into an interior office with a traditional dark wood desk and leather chairs.

> *"Our department handles everything from soup to nuts," she explained as she eased herself into a deep armchair. "I need to be present to see if the cables are being pulled in the right places and to make sure that each person who is moved gets the connections and the hardware and software they need. But with all the mergers and moves and combined offices it takes a lot of time. Top management wants it done right away, but they don't understand a thing about how complex this really is. While I am running around worrying about where the technology and furniture will go, I have to also be concerned with how and why the different versions of software from the merged companies and departments don't fit together."*

Floor plans and furniture and hardware and software compatibility are not Julia's only worries. The last merger, the sixth in her tenure, brought her bank and a brokerage firm together, and "it's not so much the different

Scott Adams, creator of the comic strip DILBERT stands in "Dilbert's Ultimate Cubicle" which includes a hammock, aquarium, rotating floor modules, shoe polisher, and a self-timing guest seat. The cubicle was designed in resonse to "thousands of readers [who] have e-mailed me with gripes about their cubicles. I feel their pain because I served a 16-year sentence in cubicles during my corporate career," said Adams. (AP Photo/Bob Riha Jr.)

computer applications, but the cultures that don't mix," she says. "Mergers and moves are a nightmare."

Julia worked her way up to vice president in the technology services division and is proud of the fact that she earns a "six-figure" salary. As a Caribbean-American woman who started her corporate rise in computer operations in the late 1980s, she is part of a women's group within the company that concerns itself with the all too opaque glass ceiling. "Conversations and decisions in the bar and the golf club are still the rule," she explains, "and pay disparities abound." The women's group meets on a regular basis, comparing notes and making plans around issues like care for aging parents, and realistic flex-time arrangements.

Flexible working hours are a double-edged sword. Julia's workweek—an incredibly fast-paced one with ten-, twelve-, and sometimes fourteen-hour days—often stretches to seven and eight days. Her family worries that her health is affected, fearing that she is working herself to death, what the Japanese call *karoshi*. And other women in her company women's group report increases in what their doctors say are stress-related illnesses. This is no small matter. A Gallop survey reported that more than 40 percent of professional and clerical workers complained about stress on a daily or close to daily basis. Similarly, the U.S. Department of Health Services reported that more than half of 40,000 workers they studied reported "a lot or a moderate amount of stress."[16]

The fast tempo and the stress are also striking in company levels far below Julia's where with each move and merger, workers are given a "choice" of remaining with the company only if they are willing to be relocated. I interviewed a large group of employees at the same bank when they were enrolled in the company-sponsored education and training program at a training center. "Job security is 'relo,'" one woman explained to me with the slang term used for "relocation." She had agreed to relocate in Texas rather than be on the "cut list." Most of the women I met, however, commented that relocation was not an option with their kids in school and the difficulty of finding new child care arrangements. Some were offered new titles within the metropolitan region, although the titles did not come with raises, and in many cases the commuting time was markedly increased. [17]

The workers, almost all of whom were women, were a technologically savvy group, having either worked with the banks' computer applications or in the IT department. Their concerns, in addition to the personal trauma of having to re-interview for their jobs, and wondering where their next "relo" might land them, focused on the software nightmare of the incompatible computer applications following each merger. Their arguments, like others I heard in similar situations in other organizations, ran along the lines of "they always promise us that it will be easier to use, but why isn't it?" and "why don't they listen to us, we know how it works."

Such comments are symptomatic of computer software applications that are built top-down by management dictate, rather than involving the workers who actually know what the systems do. Explaining how a "plain vanilla package" from one of the merged banks didn't fit in with the work practices of the other bank, a woman in the IT department elaborated on the problems: "We *have* to make it work. The vendors who supplied it aren't supporting it any longer, and the branches and the back office are using different versions." And for the workers in the remaining branch and back offices, the problems mount because as one woman explained, "We can't override the system anymore."

"Overriding the system" in their jobs, like in millions of other offices, is a common occurrence. It happens frequently when, for example, a customer calls with a problem that is not listed on the computer screen. Standard systems design practices call for computer systems to be designed by management, and as we have seen in other aspects of work, management's intent is to change work processes and to further control them. When call-center operators can't answer a customer's question this isn't considered a loss of productivity, because the computer system itself is designed to count only the transactions listed on the menu. For workers these numbers mean a lot, since performance evaluations and possible raises are based on counts of transactions. In this way, systems that can't be worked around are an additional method for monitoring workers.

According to the American Management Association, 77.7 percent of companies reported that they electronically monitored their workers on a routine basis. As Andrew Ross, author of *No-Collar: The Human Workplace and Its Hidden Costs*, put it:

> It turned out that supervision of workers' time and actions was even more systematic in the computerized workplace than it had been under the factory foreman.[18]

Through the Interface

Earlier chapters in this book have recounted how the work of people in the computer field has changed since its inception in the 1950s. Not surprisingly, the evolution of this type of knowledge work followed a similar pattern, resulting, as discussed in the opening of this chapter, in computer programming and software engineering jobs being transferred to lower-waged workers outside of industrialized countries. But how did it get this way? And why, in the lives of the people living through it, does it appear that the pace of change is increasing? In her fascinating book, *White Collar Sweatshop,* Jill Andresky Fraser argued:

It now appears that white-collar workers can be sorted into three basic categories: those whose jobs have been reengineered by technology; those who are being replaced by technology (as when nearly 180,000 bank tellers were replaced by ATMs between 1983 and 1993); and those whose lives appear—at least for now—to be resistant to such changes, typically because of the high levels of skill, experience or creativity their jobs demand.

But she goes on to explain, "That third category is small and shrinking, seemingly before our eyes."[19]

Fraser's argument, like many others, is that "new technological advances have pushed computer and other electronic capabilities far beyond the realm most people would have imagined even a decade ago."[20] While this certainly seems to match our perception, the ways that high levels of skill and creativity are squeezed out of jobs is not just through the introduction of technologies.

As with earlier waves of so-called de-skilling, computer programmers didn't necessarily lose their skill; rather it was the value and the perception of their skill that was taken away by management reorganization and dividing up labor. One of the main factors leading to the outsourcing of hundreds of thousands of IT jobs, was upper-management's belief that such moves were necessary and possible. Strategic managers seem to believe that programmers, like call-center operators, bank tellers, and other declining occupations, were expendable—at least in their own country. In 2003, a senior Microsoft vice president told an audience of managers to "pick something to move offshore today."[21] His proclamation came before realistic numbers were available on the full costs of outsourcing work, yet major corporations jumped into this fast-moving exodus of jobs.

Meanwhile, programming skills, in terms of number and range of programming languages, application tools, and Web design principles have been expanding. In the mid-1990s, for example, a programmer would have been expected to know something like HTML code and a computer language like C, but today a wide and changing range of Web tools like Dreamweaver and

Flash, along with coding languages like Pearl, C++, and JAVA, are required. Companies also require higher educational credentials including at least a bachelor's degree, rather than an associate degree, and in some areas graduate degrees in Computer Science or an M.B.A. in Information Technology.

Until recently white-collar workers were not likely to unionize. One reason for this was the notion that office workers would expect to be treated professionally and therefore didn't think they needed union protection. But another reason was the strong reluctance on the part of the entrenched, largely white-male industrial unions to organize office workers, who were, for the most part, better educated and different from them. Now, however, union organizing of professional and technical workers is heating up as these workers are brought into the de-skilling model of industrial work and as unions wake up to these expanding segments of the labor force. The Communication Workers of America (CWA) has made inroads among Technical, Office and Professional (TOP) workers, particularly in the high-tech Seattle area, and the Professional Employees department of the AFL-CIO, representing 4 million technical, professional, and skilled white-collar workers—is putting on a nationwide push for organizing technical and professional workers. An AFL-CIO report entitled "The Professional and Technical Work Force: A New Frontier for Unions," argues that while blue-collar unionism is declining with the continuing drop in the number of factory workers, "professional specialists," including technical workers, are the fastest-growing part of the labor force.[22] As we will see in the next section, these jobs are not expanding at anywhere near the rate projected at the end of the twentieth century.

Similarly, legal actions like one by IBM employees around the loss of their secure pension benefits resulted in an employee association affiliated with the Communication Workers of America (CWA)—an unthinkable notion only a decade ago. And the class-action lawsuit by temporary workers at Microsoft—called "permatemps" by those in the IT field—restricted the way Microsoft hires and treats its contingent workers. Union struggles are also following outsourced IT work. In an interesting twist in Ireland, for example, unionized Bank of Ireland IT employees threatened a strike in order to head off the bank's plans to outsource computer work to the

American firm Hewlett-Packard (HP), which had bid to manage all of the bank's networks and computer systems.[23]

Un-, Under- and Differently Employed

Economists and government analysts in industrialized nations around the globe point to the remarkably low unemployment rate in the United States as an example of how a successful flexible labor market should work. In particular, government analysts pushing newer "market liberalization" strategies in Eastern Europe and South America claim that the U.S. unemployment rate of between 5.5 and 6.5 percent is an indication that removing government regulations and doing away with labor union rules results in a healthy and growing economy. What is not mentioned, however, is the fact that the official U.S. rate is based on only a sample of households *self-reporting* their employment—unlike Canada, Australia, and other developed countries which have much higher rates of unemployment based on actual unemployment claims. Nor is the issue of what the unemployment rate leaves out discussed.

Every month the Bureau of Labor Statistics conducts a telephone survey of 60,000 sampled households in the United States asking respondents if they worked or looked for work during the previous week. This sample is then used to project an estimated number for the entire labor force. Not included in the working population are the 1.5 million "discouraged workers"—people who have stopped actively looking for work. Another group left out consists of those who have retired or just dropped out of the labor market. There are no official statistics for this group, but all reports indicate that the number of people who are taking early retirement or saying that they are retired when they can no longer find work is increasing rapidly.[24]

Also hidden behind the numbers are the almost five million part-time workers who say that they want to be working full-time, the so-called underemployed. Another group, and a rapidly emerging presence, is the close to 10 million people in "alternative work arrangements" who say they are self-employed. If these categories were included in the unemployment statistics, as they are more likely to be in other countries, the unemployment rate in the United States would be approximately 10 percent, similar to that of other economies.[25] Other economists put the number at over 12 percent if the rate were to also include the underemployed.[26]

The fault with the U. S. statistics is not so much a sin of commission but one of omission, based on earlier notions of who is in the workforce. Up until the economic shake-ups in the 1990s, when the so-called New Economy came into being, employment data could somewhat reliably be counted by surveying the household samples and by collecting data from company payrolls. But these models were based on the idea that being employed meant being on the payroll of one employer. The increases in the number of contingent and alternative work arrangements now being reported by the Bureau of Labor Statistics reflect the shift away from employment in one place for a predictable period of time. The strong work ethic among American workers points to the possibility that people *say* that they are employed even if they are not. It is also probable that many people reporting themselves as temporary workers, part-time, or self-employed are seriously underemployed. From a societal perspective this results in the wasted potential of millions of people, and on an individual level it causes emotional pain along with sudden drops in income and loss of health insurance.

Meanwhile, by all accounts people who are employed are working longer hours. Over 25 million workers reported that they spend more than forty-nine hours a week working.[27] In professional and technical jobs in particular, the working day has intensified by expectations of working through lunch and doubling up on work tasks. And if the workday is not actually extended in the office, the need to stay connected via mobile phone, Personal Digital Assistants (PDAs) such as Blackberries, and Internet connections has also lengthened the working day. A Bureau of Labor Statistics special supplement in May 2001 reported that 25 million Americans worked from home for some amount of time.[28] Workers in administrative support positions are also experiencing stretched-out and intensified workdays as lunch breaks are shortened in order to get tasks done. While e-mail was a boon to people in administrative support positions in its early days, now workers report that just catching up on e-mail creates more work than they can handle in an eight-hour workday. Many people blame themselves for being inefficient in their use of time. It is not the time that is the problem, however, but rather the expectation that more tasks, including e-mail, returned phone calls, reports, spreadsheets, meetings, and conference arrangements need to get done.[29]

Hidden in Plain Sight

While the media reports the number of jobs slipping out of the country and the number of workers retiring, there is surprisingly little about the fact that we, the consumers, are doing our own unpaid labor. Remember a time when you didn't order tickets online? Or prescriptions? Or clothes? And remember a time when you called a doctor's office or an insurance company and got a person on the phone instead of a command to press "0" to speak to a person. There are no reliable statistics on how much daily-living work is actually being done at home or at work by people trying to arrange their lives. But by all accounts people are spending far more time than they had planned to buying, scheduling, or otherwise organizing their daily lives via the Web or through automated telephone systems. These Web and telephone systems are designed to cut down on the number of employed workers by shunting non-paid work onto the shoulders of everyone.

In *The Making of a Cybertariat*, Ursula Huws lays out the logic of how consumption is turned into work.[30] In buying goods and services through the Web we are ordering services that have been turned into commodities, propelling new forms of consumer behavior. Interestingly, she notes that the way we consume goods and services through automated systems is "leading to a Taylorization of private life."[31] In her view, it is not just jobs that are made more routine, but the very way we search the Web and press buttons for telephone orders that routinizes our daily life.

Back in 1988, Barbara Garson explained how jobs were being made more routine in *The Electronic Sweatshop*. She analyzed how a script was developed for reservation clerks at an airline that "had divided the two-minute reservation conversation into segments—opening, sales pitch, probe, and close—and provided a set of interchangeable conversation modules for each segment."[32]

Today it would be hard to find a website or a telephone system that veers from this model. People trying to discuss problems on the telephone about their telephone bill, mortgage, rent, insurance payment, etc., report having to press what seems to be an endless series of numbers before they can get the information they need. And the same is said of website navigation: the category one is looking for is often not there or very hard to find. Just like the complaint that bank workers have about not being able to work around the computer system, consumers find that their unpaid labor is a great deal of work as they try to find ways around company websites or phone systems to get to a human being.

Where we are actually sitting when we do the work of daily living is also problematic, as more and more people find they run into problems if they spend too much time online at home and have problems getting work done if they let their personal business spill over to the office computer or phone. The traditional line between public and private space is also visibly blurred in terms of the way we experience the places where we do this additional work. People I spoke to told of moving the computer from the living room to the bedroom, only to find that it angered a spouse, or that they were upset to find themselves online in the middle of the night. One woman said that she had found the perfect place by making a "nest for myself" when she moved her computer into a closet.

Home is becoming a contested terrain, since computers are used in almost any room for multiple purposes, including unpaid labor like ordering food and arranging appointments, and entertainment. While we experience home as a place to work, play, and carry out the chores of daily life, the way these activities are done is reshaping our sense of home as a place. Dolores Hayden, an urban planner who has written extensively about place, says that "*place* is one of the trickiest words in the English language, a suitcase so overfilled one can never shut the lid."[33] Place is different from the broader term *space* because it carries with it the meanings, memories, attachments, and identity we connect with places. In *The Power of Place*, Hayden, like geographer Henri Lefebvre, argues for under standing place as the production of space—a process that is economic, political and social.

There is little research about how we experience a sense of place when we are navigating in cyberspace (a term coined in William Gibson's 1984 novel *Neuromancer*). But we do know where we are when we are sitting at a computer or holding a phone. And that place may no longer be simply "home" or work but in-between areas that we carve out as we overlap many tasks. Architects are beginning to take the question of home/work space more seriously in home design.[34]

While parts of many homes are beginning to look more like workplaces, some companies are trying to add features to make work spaces look like home. Office spaces often include kitchenettes with refrigerators and microwave ovens, and now some organizations are also putting in on-site washing machines, dry cleaners, workout rooms, and child care services. Many upper-level managers have showers and dressing rooms, and some companies even offer personal training services and massages. These more homelike features are added because professional and managerial employees complain that they do not have enough time to get out during the week to take care of everything.[35]

Most automated systems—phone or computer—promise to "serve the customer better" and "to save time," yet few people are fooled when they end up spending more time searching for something on the Web or waiting on hold to speak to an actual person. True, there is a great deal of information available on the Web, from weather to train and flight schedules, hotels, car rentals, and film schedules. But the list of daily chores and the time it takes to do them seems to grow exponentially as more and more information is put online or embedded into automated telephone systems.

It's interesting to see that the telecommuting forecasts of the 1980s (work from home but still connected to an office) and the virtual office talk of the 1990s (work from a temporary time-shared cubicle) have morphed into a more hybrid sense of home/office/work/transit/consumer space. Yet, hidden in plain sight, is the fact that as the tempo of each activity picks up and blends in with other activities we need to look carefully at not just the changes in the physical division of labor we are experiencing but at the way our physical environments are merging. As I have reported throughout this book, researchers have studied the way work has been reorganized and technology designed to speed and blend work practices. But the newer forms of working arrangements need far more study in terms of where and when they are done and how they coexist with multiple activities. All pre-liminary evidence points to increased stress levels, at home, at work, and on the road. And while these hybrid life activities and the places they are done from all appear to spring out of increased use of mobile technologies (phone, laptops, Palm devices, and the like), the technologies themselves were designed to support reorganized work/lives. What we can do about these changes is everyone's business.

8. Shaking off False Assumptions

The immunity from global competition that U.S. white-collar employees have enjoyed for so long has started to vanish.
                              —*Business Week*, March 2004[1]

In the book *Alice in Wonderland*, Alice falls down a rabbit hole and finds a
world that seems to follow different rules and based on different assumptions. To many workers the workplace changes described here sounds as if
we might have fallen into a similarly warped world. But we have the advantage
of deciphering the assumptions that propel the economic changes we are
experiencing. And by understanding the assumptions we can peel away the
hype about the supposed technological wizardry of our age and look at how
the economic rules work. This chapter concludes with an overview of this
analysis and some examples about what people are doing to change things.

In one of the interviews I conducted for this book I felt like a cousin of
Alice falling into my own rabbit hole. I entered a world where computer
systems were being designed for transporting the electronic symbols we call
money around the world. It was a rarefied environment, high up in an
office tower, with sleeker and better-designed cubicles and open conference
rooms looking down on the city. This was the backbone of interbank monetary transfer, which provides the infrastructure for business-to-business
(B2B) and electronic commerce (e-commerce). Whiteboards were filled
with organizational scribbling, detailing how new versions of the software
and the network infrastructure should work, although I couldn't understand any of the arcane language.

The company was in the final stages of putting together specifications for a new version of the system. These specifications would then be sent out for bids from software companies all over the world. In the last round of contracts, a large Indian software consulting firm had won a major share of the consortium contract and had, in turn, outsourced segments of the software development to smaller firms in other countries.[2]

The software encoded interbank transfer messages and confirmations about electronic monetary transfers. Today's rapidly moving global economy, frequently referred to as the new or frictionless economy, purportedly is made up out of the immaterial gossamer web of electronic commerce. Yet it is very much rooted in the material conditions of labor markets and labor processes, just as were its predecessors.

The value of software code and information in databases, whether sold as shrink-wrapped packages in stores to consumers or custom designed, like the interbank system, comes from the labor that develops it. The living labor of people using information technology and the embedded, or fixed, labor of the applications and infrastructure they use combine to powerfully push up the tempo of working and daily life.

The previous chapters in this book have looked at how changes in labor processes and labor markets have unfolded, particularly in the United States. We now set the whirlwind of these job changes within three major global economic changes.

1. *Global economy:* The phenomenon commonly called globalization encompasses a worldwide redivision of labor. As work processes in different industries were specialized and standardized into smaller pieces of work, like those in computer programming, these specialized tasks were increasingly divided among countries and regions in the world. This is part of what economists call *flexible accumulation,* because it means that both capital and labor can be flexibly divided up and parceled out among different workforces. The current form of flexible accumulation is based on something mainstream economists call *market liberalization,* which involves removing governmental barriers to the "free flow" of labor.

2. Commodification of services: For much of the twentieth century, economists and business managers argued that services were not open to the same division of labor as tangible products, such as automobiles, because services involved nonquantifiable professional and administrative labor. But by the 1970s and 1980s major employment sectors like finance (banking), insurance, real estate, and law, were turning services into products that could then be sold as commodities. These commodities—everything from computer programs for designing kitchens to bank transactions—could then be made and sold in many countries. They also could be produced more quickly and cheaply as the labor processes of creating them were being made more productive.

3. Digital exchange: Twenty-twenty hindsight lets us see how the changes in labor processes, coupled with computer technology in the second half of the twentieth century, were slowly but surely making a paper-based economy into a digital one. The digital infrastructure of the global economy is not, however, the so-called new economy promised in the 1990s, nor is it the paperless office predicted in the 1980s. Digital exchange is built on labor processes that have been divided into pieces and these pieces carved out into products. Now, fifty years after the birth of the computer age, the exchange of products and labor is increasingly supported by an electronic infrastructure rather than paper documents or paper money.

The following illustrates these points by way of describing how IT labor processes have been transformed into software and computer chips. In some ways this combination of changing production and changing technology is not very different from the processes that Karl Marx described in the early industrial period.

Constant revolutionizing of production, uninterrupted disturbance of all social conditions, everlasting uncertainty and agitation distinguish the bourgeois epoch from all earlier ones. All fixed, fast frozen relations, with their train of ancient and venerable prejudices and opinions, are swept away, all new-formed ones become antiquated before they can ossify. All that is solid melts into air, all that is holy is profaned, and man is at last compelled to face with sober senses his real condition of life and his relations with his kind.[3]

Solid Labor into Software

The software and computer chips that power electronic technologies, be they mobile telephones, Palm devices, laptops, or complete information systems, are built by labor. Earlier chapters described how each step of the labor process of creating programs has been specialized, routinized, and divided from other parts of the software production process. While computer programming in the 1960s was largely a craft, procedural programming languages like COBOL were introduced to speed up code production. By the late 1970s data-processing management experts had something called structured programming in place with the hope of reorganizing programming work so that managers could better control it.[4]

Easier-to-use programming languages coupled with routine coding procedures resulted in a devaluation of programming skill, so that by the early 1990s programmers' salaries were no longer rising as they had been. During this period another significant change took place: computer programs were written as packaged products to be sold on the market, thus making it possible for consumers and businesses to buy off-the-shelf software.

Additionally, object-oriented programming languages like JAVA (named for the coffee programmers drank trying to keep awake) and C++ were gaining popularity. These languages, markedly different from the earlier procedural languages and the structured code that supported them, were designed to integrate databases with software routines. This meant that each "object" of information from a database, such as a name, Social Security number, and address, could be used in any number of different programs without programmers having to recode it.[5]

This broad-brush overview of changes in the software labor process leaves out many of the contradictions of confused management policies that often took things backward before moving them forward. As described in chapters 4 and 5, strategic management employed different forms of centralizing and decentralizing organizations, leaving problems in their wake. This is still going on. Currently, for example, organizations claim that they are decentralizing work and decision making through centralized databases and so-called data warehousing, where all electronic databases are linked together for management access.

These centralized data warehouse operations give management the illusion of being close to office-floor decision making, but they can only rely on decisions as presented through the data—and all workers know that what happens at work is not really represented in the statistics management gets fed. Additionally, these centralized databases not only leave organizations open to the kinds of security breaches that IT magazines fret about, but they also create major problems if anything goes wrong in any part of their worldwide operations. The house of decentralized organizations is built on the cards of centralized data files.

The meteoric rise of Internet use in the late 1990s brought with it an increased need for new types of programming and IT work.[6] Yet this last period mimics the earlier periods, although in faster motion. In fact, the new media field of the late 1990s now seems like a blur of programmers doing some Web design, graphic designers doing some programming, and "content providers" (publishing companies, entertainment firms, and business organizations, etc.) writing the material that gets viewed on the Web. All of which leaves the door open to another round of cutting jobs into specialized parts, devaluing skills, reorganizing work, and packaging services and software as new products. A special edition on new technology in *Business Week* summarizes it this way:

> Only a decade ago, writing computer code and software-application maintenance were considered complex and secure ways for aspiring Americans to make a living. Now, it's considered "rote work" and companies such as Microsoft Corp. and Netscape Communications Corp. have it done everywhere from Ireland to India.[7]

Confronting Conventional Wisdom

Much of the way we look at work, jobs, organizations, technology, and the economy is presented—in schools, at home, in the media, and in management literature—as conventional wisdom: sets of ideas that seem to be common sense. In what follows, we will examine the developments described in earlier chapters in the wider context of economic and political policy in order to challenge what passes for common sense. The world we

Does work have to look like this? [Jim West]

experience is neither the technological utopia the popular media touts, nor the dystopia that so many critics claim.[8]

In the 1950s and 1960s, conventional wisdom claimed that the computer age would bring with it an information industry that would employ increasing numbers of well-paid white-collar workers. The message was spiced up in the 1970s and 1980s with a dash of high-tech dressing: technology would bring with it high-skill jobs that would be rewarded with high pay. Technology in general, and computers in particular, would bring forth a new future.

But as we have seen, conventional wisdom, particularly as presented through the nonanalytical lens of the popular media, is not always what it seems. Take, for example, the period from the 1950s through the 1980s, when office jobs were expanding. The office sector was creating enough jobs to offset the diminishing factory sector. We were told that this growth was fueled by the expansion of businesses that were competing effectively, even though much of it was the result of military and government spending. Even in the 1980s, despite the Reagan cutbacks, public sector jobs declined very little and military expenditures continued to support industrial companies with large white-collar payrolls, like Boeing Aircraft.

By the 1990s, there was no longer any magic pin holding office sector jobs in place. Political pressure to cut government spending, reinforced by workplace reengineering, not only "displaced" workers temporarily, but the link between jobs and secure employment was permanently cut. Even as military budgets continue to expand, increasing proportions of these expenditures are going to outsourced contractors.

The vestiges of the old, factory-style division of labor and the early, automated data-processing systems can still be seen in many jobs today, primarily because management policies—both the old-style "bureaucratic" and newer, so-called humanistic ones[9]—laid the foundation for the separation between the head and the hands, and between the workplace and the worker. In other words, the "head" of company decision making has been separated from the "hands" that do the work anywhere, as we saw in software work.

These versions of conventional wisdom rest on the belief that business leaders know what is best for us, and this in turn is rooted in the assumption that unrestrained capitalist growth, supported by science and technology, will automatically lead to growing economies, and to more and better jobs for those who are prepared for them. But as we saw in the previous chapters, this is no more than a corporate and technological leap of faith. After all, increased profits—the engine of growth—are the result of management's ability to decrease overall labor costs and make the labor process more controllable. Thus, more competitive labor markets force workers to compete against one another and thereby hold wages down. And more streamlined labor processes, which press people to work harder and produce more quantifiable output, stand in stark contrast to the notion that increased competition is good for workers.

Capitalism as an economic system is built on the premise that it must continue to expand to new markets to sell new products and find cheaper sources of labor. The globalization under way today extends that concept by further dividing up labor between countries. Not that this is new. Prior to the nineteenth century European ships steamed their way to Asian ports to bring back expertly woven fabrics as well as hauling hand-crafted carpets from South and Central Asia and the Middle East and Africa.[10] Early capitalism created a financial base, in part, on a foundation of trade by importing then superior quality products made by specialized laborers around the world. European industrial production in the nineteenth century seized the trade advantage by more rapidly producing goods and selling them as commodities around the globe.

Division of labor in earlier expansionist periods had the effect of creating an unequal distribution of goods and incomes around the world and within countries. This remains true today. According to a report by a World Bank economist, "The richest 1 percent of people in the world gets as much income as the poorest 57 percent."[11] Extreme poverty is pervasive among the majority of the world's population. Income inequality continues to follow in the wake of this unequal distribution of work and money. For example, the increase in new jobs in both India and China has been accompanied by an increase in income inequality in both countries, with the wealth of a comparative few far outstripping the subsistence and marginal incomes of the majority.[12] In the United States, income and tax disparities are glaring. Paul Krugman, a popular and prolific economist, has estimated that 70 percent of the income growth in the expansionist 1980s went to only 1 percent of the population.[13] Mounting evidence points to a huge disparity between the increased taxes middle- and lower-income Americans pay and the declining taxes paid by wealthy Americans and by corporations.[14]

Inequality and poverty are one terrible part of the expansionist equation. The consequences of unrestrained expansion are having disastrous consequences for peoples and governments in countries where market liberalization is enforced through U.S. pressure and through the World Trade Organization.[15] This is certainly not the scenario presented by business leaders when they intone the mantra of market liberalization. They claim that such policies set about to "free" business from the "shackles" of government regulation. The mounting worldwide protests against meetings of the World Trade Organization illustrate the point that people notice when government regulations are removed from corporations and corporations are free to operate outside of laws and public scrutiny.[16]

Competitive Vs. Collective Action

Capitalism, a competitive system to its core, must put profits ahead of people, and reinforce competitive values in people to get them to jump after jobs, even in the face of huge income inequalities. The language of competition, combined with the ideology of individualism and professionalism, keeps workers, particularly office workers, divided. Workers who believe that they must "work hard to get ahead" are pressured to constantly upgrade their skills, and as they work harder and harder, they may fail to notice that they, like millions of others, have been shunted off to a side trail—no longer part of an upwardly mobile path to increased wages. Instead of blaming their managers, or their companies, or an economic system geared to make people compete, many workers end up blaming themselves. Yet at various points in recent history a critical mass of people have banded together to bring about change.

In order to confront the survival-of-the-fittest mentality of unrestrained capitalism, a number of progressive patterns of work relations were established in industrialized countries. In the United States, social movements in the 1930s and 1940s won Social Security for retired workers, unemployment insurance for laid-off workers, and public assistance for a wide range of people who couldn't work or didn't make enough to support themselves or their families. In 1965, after people pressured Congress, Medicaid and Medicare were introduced to provide health care for poor and low-waged people and for senior citizens. Following the Second World War, unions were able to win higher wages and better health insurance, which the government and businesses agreed to help finance as long as the unions didn't demand wider changes—such as a voice in deciding technology or participation in management decisions.

Unlike other industrialized countries, however, where labor-oriented governments brought some management rights and privileges under union control, in the past American white-collar workers were not open to unionization or much in the way of collective action. Perhaps this was due in part to the fact that the white-collar middle class seemed, according to media pronouncements, more interested in upward mobility—as promised by the various technological and information revolutions—than in fighting for workplace rights. As corporate employees, they bargained individually with their managers for higher salaries and annual increases. The belief was that if you were good, you would get ahead—an assumption built on the faith that office workers would be generously compensated for the skills they had acquired through education and experience. Although a large number of people were able to enter corporate, professional, and government jobs during the period of economic expansion, it took social policy in the form of affirmative action to pry open office doors for a wider range of workers, including women and minorities.[17]

In the early part of the twentieth century, at the height of the industrial period, workers organized unions to fight for the collective rights of people working under one factory roof; these were later expanded into industry-wide unions, such as the AFL-CIO in the United States, and country-wide unions in other industrial countries. In the 1960s and 1970s, the beginning of the postindustrial period, people in the United States fought for and won major civil rights in the midst of a rapidly changing economy.[18] Now, as we enter yet another period of major upheaval, it is an open question whether corporate short-term profit taking can continue unchecked. The question is relevant for both managers and workers. For managers, the reengineering process has created a workforce that owes no particular allegiance to a given workplace or employer; for workers, the heightened competition has affected health and the ability to spend time outside of work. The urgency of this problem makes it especially necessary to ask new questions and plan new courses of action.

The notion of individualism is particularly prevalent in the United States. The image of the rugged individual carrying out his or her "advancement" was probably never applicable to the office worker—or any other worker, for that matter—but it continues to be used today. Individualism as an ideology has the effect of heightening competition among people and isolating them. It is having a media rebirth now, as part of the rush to encourage young people to become entrepreneurs—the ultimate image of the individual out there on his or her own. The worldwide media myths about computer hackers as lonely individuals writing programs for the good (shareware and open source software) or for evil (breaking into computer systems) are very much a continuation of this cult of the individual, although it is clear to IT professionals that the hacker community has been banding together against corporate domination.[19] While there is nothing wrong with a person trying to do his or her best and expecting to be rewarded for it, the problem is that individualism and professionalism are being bent out of shape, used primarily for the benefit of the organization, not the worker or the customer.

It's not as if Americans are completely overwhelmed by the cult of individualism, of course. Outside of the workplace, Americans have a rich history of group action, from struggles over the environment to successful movements for women's rights, civil rights, and immigrant rights. In schools, neighborhoods, communities, towns, cities, and regions, the track record of fighting to better communities is undeniable. What is unusual in the United States is that while this spirit of cooperative and collective action has been successful in changing civil laws in public society, it has not tackled the right of management to control lives at work.

Sociologists and anthropologists who study workplaces tell us that most work is done collectively, and that most office workers not only prefer to work together, but need to cooperate in order to accomplish such seemingly "routine" tasks as fixing the copier when paper jams happen.[20] Office work, like most work, is by its very nature cooperative, and information workers, with their heavy dependency on new versions of software, databases, and new equipment, need to rely on one another to figure out how things work. We have all found out that asking a coworker a question about how to use some features in a new software version or how to transfer a message on a voice-mail system, are the best ways to get something done. Many people reported that their first attempt at using Windows menus would have been nerve-racking without a coworker leaning over their shoulder. We rely on each other for all sorts of information that makes our jobs more interesting and more productive. Yet this human web of cooperation disappears when office workers individually ask for salary increases or more flexible work arrangements.

C. Wright Mills wrote that technical and managerial jobs were built on the false assumption that the workers who held those jobs would inherit power in the office. He noted that moving up from the lower ranks of a corporate hierarchy was no more automatic than it had been for the working class in the industrial period.[21] The linking of knowledge-based work with possible power is a purposely constructed illusion: the phrase "knowledge is power" does not translate into higher wages or better working conditions. Collectively shaking off these false assumptions and reexamining some of the strong cooperative actions we take in our daily lives may keep us from getting trapped in a future where we each have to bargain for some small piece of work—a world of individual freelancers competing against one another.

Taking a page out of C. Wright Mills's 1951 description of the enormous file of an office, Ursula Huws portrays an updated picture of the world-wide homogenization of work:

> Meanwhile, across the rest of the workforce an extraordinary and unprecedented convergence has been taking place. From tele-sales staff to typesetters, from indexers to insurance underwriters, from librarians to ledger clerks, from planning inspectors to pattern-cutters, a large and increasing proportion of daily work time is spent identically: sitting with one hand poised over a keyboard and the other dancing back and forth from keys to mouse.[22]

Popular culture and the rich genre of cyber fiction also portray many of the changes described in this book. *Snow Crash*, by the prolific writer Neil Stephenson, reveals programming history through his main character:

> When Hiro learned how to do this, way back fifteen years ago, a hacker could sit down and write an entire piece of software by himself. Now, that's no longer possible. Software comes out of factories, and hackers are, to a greater or lesser extent, assembly-line workers. Worse yet, they may become managers who never get to write any code themselves.[23]

Opening Windows

Other postindustrial economies are doing things differently. Labor governments in the period after World War II pushed for worker-oriented rights to be included in government programs of social protection. These sometimes socialist movements put some checks and balances on freewheeling capitalist economies from Europe to Australia, to South America, Africa, and of course Canada. The European Union, for example, has a Social Contract as part of its 1991 charter guaranteeing certain rights to working people. The U.S. Constitution, which fiercely guards individual freedoms, has no provisions that protect its citizens when they enter the workplace or contract with an employer.

Most European countries guarantee access to free higher education, some form of paid parental leave, and government-insured health care. In most industrialized nations, education is financed and protected by the national governments. Yet in the United States, as taxes are reduced and funding slashed at local levels, the gap between rich and poor school districts has widened, threatening the education of more and more working-class and minority students, as well as affecting the education of middle-class youth. Government proposals to increase funding for job training miss the point entirely, as workers are not so much in need of specific training for specific jobs. The worldwide redistribution of work, and the temporary nature of most jobs, only increases the importance of broad-based education that strengthens critical thinking.

In the nineteenth and early twentieth centuries, public and private organizations in the United States built a transportation infrastructure of railroads and trolley car lines. In New York City, for example, the subway was considered an important link for bringing workers inexpensively and effectively to and from their jobs. Now, however, the emphasis is moving away from public transportation and toward building highways for cars and the information superhighway for telecommunications. Both of these favor privately contracted infrastructure over public or mass facilities. In Europe and Japan, on the other hand, governments support revitalized rail transport, local public transportation systems, and publicly financed fiber-optic networks, although these nations are now also turning to the private financing model favored by market liberalization..

Perhaps the most glaring difference between the United States and its close economic competitors is its lack of free and universal health care. While conservatives argue that Americans shouldn't lose the right to a "free choice of doctors," other nations have had comprehensive medical plans for several decades. In Scandinavian countries, free eye exams and occupational and physical therapy are provided for people using computers.

Most of the public policy debates about health care in the United States focus on employer-based insurance. Given the overwhelming labor market changes in the last decade it is now clearly absurd to assume that insurance should be tied to a single employer. This is early-twentieth-century industrial thinking rooted in the notion that workers were to be paternalistically protected by their employers within the walls of a single workplace. The same outdated employer-sponsored model also hinders policy around paid family leave, sick leave, and pensions.

To be sure, in the U.S., more and more people are clamoring for single-payer insurance systems, but companies are still caught up in the illogic of believing that they can bind workers to jobs by controlling benefits. At a time when corporations and government agencies continue to cut workers on payroll, and as workers are urged to "think outside of the box" and go out on their own, the only alternative that makes sense for both workers and management is recognizing that humane supportive benefits need to be treated as a societal cost, not an individual one. If conservatives who advocate family values were to really put into practice such collective values, they too would argue for society to support maternity/paternity leave, paid time for taking care of older family members, and health coverage for all.

Associations and unions like those of actors, musicians, and writers—perpetual freelance workers—have banded together to provide their members with ongoing health insurance. Likewise, many temporary staffing agencies offer health coverage for people they employ. Independent associations of freelancers in many cities are also moving in this direction. The American government and large corporations, stuck in conservative thinking that advocates limited governmental services, steadfastly fight against this obvious need for public health care.

Decisions about technology in the workplace are another point of departure. Under Australia's Labor government in the 1990s, the government undertook revamping the tax collection system, by involving representatives from the 18,000-member Taxation Office. This form of more bottom-up participatory action involved redesigning jobs, developing new forms of work organization, and creating new information systems. The public service employees union was included in the decision making and, along with labor-oriented systems consultants, helped keep the project focused on the work that actually took place in the offices—not on management's version of what they thought should happen.

In Scandinavia, where the right of employees to "co-determine" technology policy dates back to the 1970s, laws and supported workshops give workers the right to determine what type of technology should be used in the workplace. This can take many forms, including unions and workers hiring their own consultants and choosing their own educational programs, but most important, co-determination boils down to the idea that hardware and software should not be introduced in a workplace unless the workers agree to it.

Until recently, unions in the United States failed to organize most of the office sector. There are many reasons for this, including the fact that American trade unions were based on the older bureaucratic industrial model and failed to see the important growth of service-sector workers—particularly minority and women workers. Organizing white-collar workers was never an easy task because large multinational white-collar employers like IBM had strict anti-union policies that were reinforced by emphasizing individual bargaining and making a cult of individualism and professionalism.[24] Except for government employees, most white-collar workers in the United States are not yet unionized, although, as we saw in the last chapter, this area is now a central focus for many American unions. In the European Union, where almost all workers are represented by unions and/or worker councils, bargaining occurs not only with specific employers but also across the board in order to establish and maintain country-wide rights.

Collective bargaining, while tied up in thousands of industrial-based rules and regulations, presents an important contrast to individualism. As its name implies, it is based on the idea that collectives, or groups of people, have potentially more clout than individuals, particularly when it comes to negotiations over salaries, benefits, and working conditions. The lone individual going to his or her boss and asking for a raise based on individual performance stands little chance compared to groups collectively arguing for better pay and conditions. The corporate emphasis on team and group work is indeed strangely out of sync with the cult of individualism, yet individualism continues to prevail in the workplace because employers want to keep it that way. Since most office workers bargain for themselves without knowing what their coworkers earn, the organization holds the cards.

The old industrial style of unions that based their organizing strength on the power of workers in one factory or workplace may not be the answer for collective bargaining in the rapidly changing office sector today. And European white-collar unions, with their history of national collective action, may not be an appropriate response to the long American tradition of local action, or the recent outsourcing of jobs around the globe. There are other alternatives, however, involving a collection of previously tried strategies, such as the European worker councils for local actions and international unions for worldwide action. Waitresses in the United States in the 1930s had a strong association that trained and provided workers for the vast restaurant industry. Such a model has been employed more recently for musicians, actors, writers, and other freelance occupations where workers have banded together to collectively protect their interests. And on a political level, some groups have been suggesting that employee or worker lobbies, in addition to union lobbies, be formed to counteract the power of corporate employer lobbies that now dominate Washington. Worldwide environmental action groups and public health advocacy organizations along with civil and minority rights coalitions are showing ways to new forms of organization. As are anti-World Trade Organization activists.

Whatever strategies we adopt to reshape worker-management relations, it is clear that a worker's right to healthy, safe working conditions and a living wage must be negotiated within a framework that rebalances the power of workers against the growing power of employers. In a country that proclaims itself as the "democratic leader of the free world," it is an ironic tragedy that democracy stops at the office door. A government study in the 1990s found that more than 80 percent of workers wanted to have some say in the decisions that affect their jobs and in how their work is performed.[25] The market liberalization policies that water down existing occupational safety and health regulations (which are set by OSHA in the United States) or take away legislation that protects unions and workers are not only a step backward, but seriously endanger the millions of people working from outside of traditional workplaces and outside of traditional employer-employee contractual agreements.

Clearly, we can't go backward. Instead we must build on the collective practices that have been successfully used in the past. We are bombarded with a conventional wisdom that makes it appear that technological revolutions and free-market business policies will lead to a better future. In the twenty-first century, we have had a glimpse of this future and it has not been designed for or by us. But, as our counterparts in earlier periods of major economic change have shown, we too can influence the direction of change. The more we as workers and citizens collectively question the way things are, the more possibilities there will be for us to shape the way things could be, from the technology we use to the way we organize our work and the times and places we choose to work.

Postscript

The filing cabinet metaphor adapted by the designers of the Windows operating system is, from many perspectives, a strange one. Microsoft's use of file folders and a trash basket was, to put it kindly, borrowed from the Apple Macintosh interface. The design principles of the Mac graphical user interface (GUI) borrowed heavily in turn on a mouse-driven graphical system prototyped by the Xerox Corporation in the early 1980s.

Originally Xerox and Apple adapted the office file cabinet metaphor as their central design concept in order to sell computers to organizations. Desktop or microcomputers at that time were primarily used in homes and for young children in schools. So the file cabinet metaphor, in the shape of easy to understand icons, was a step in the direction of corporate users. Or so they thought.

From the beginning, Windows was riddled with contradictions: file cabinets and trash cans are not found on top of desks; turning off a computer by pulling on the Start menu seemed illogical to thinking users; and, ironically, the computers were introduced as part of the so-called paperless office—one not requiring file cabinets at all.

Today the metaphor of file cabinets is further muddled by the fact that young people who have grown up using computers have never really relied on papers filed in cabinets. Indeed, youth have the most exposure to desktop computers in homes where filing is probably a lost art. While it is certainly true that on any given day one can find people wandering the isles of the big office-supply chains like Staples and Office Max looking for furniture and supplies to better organize their lives, file cabinets are not the hottest selling item, to say the least.

The title of this book and the cover design have certain tongue-in-cheek qualities. *Windows on the Workplace* is, of course, a play on the ubiquitous Microsoft operating system. Ursula Huws has this to say about people sitting in front of the operating system:

> Facing these workers on the screen, framed in pseudo bas relief, are ugly gray squares labeled, in whatever the local language, "File," "Edit," "View," Tools," Format," "Window," and "Help," the ghastly spoor of some aesthetically challenged Microsoft employee of the late 1990s.[1]

Windows is, of course, marketed to organizations that place it on computers in cubicles that lack windows that look out on the world. The wondrous file cabinets lying on their sides on the cover of this book similarly reflect a world slightly at odds with the one we experience. Both symbols, the window and the file cabinet, are reflective ways of looking at the world with the intent of challenging the assumptions that surround us.

Notes

Preface

1. There is a rich body of literature on technology determinism. See, for example: M. R. Smith and L. Marx, *Does Technology Drive History?* (Cambridge, MA: MIT Press, 1998) for a general overview, and Michael Adas, *Machines as the Measure of Men* (Ithaca, NY: Cornell University Press, 1989) for an analysis of how the Eurocentric perspective on technological advances reinforced the exploits of colonialism. Also, for an analysis of how technology gets its religious wrapping see Neil Postman, *Technopoly* (New York: Vintage, 1993).
2. Interviews were conducted in person, using a semi-structured interview guide. Thirty-five individual interviews were conducted in work environments, fifteen were carried out at the interviewee's request outside of the workplace, and another twenty were conducted among groups of workers. In order to protect their privacy, names of the interviewees have been changed and no names are given to the specific company for which they work. Wherever possible I have attempted to follow up on the workers I interviewed for the first edition of the book. The situated interviews allowed for a better understanding of just how work and technology actually fit together in the context of the working environment, a subject that is part of my ongoing research.

1. Introduction: Through the Looking Glass

1. Doug is not his real name. The names of individuals and companies have been changed or omitted to ensure privacy for those interviewed. Unless otherwise specified, the stories and anecdotes are based on situated interviewed described in the Preface. The interviewees were selected to represent different occupational categories, firm sizes, and employment relations. Wherever possible follow-up interviews were conducted by telephone or e-mail. In addition, I interviewed fifteen high-level managers from different types of large firms, including telecommunications, computers, banks, and staffing agencies. The survey cannot be considered statistically representa-

tive of today's white collar-occupations, but it was designed on the basis of an analysis of available Bureau of Labor Statistics data and literature for these occupations.

2. See Andrew Ross, *No-Collar:The Humane Workplace and Its Hidden Costs* (New York: Basic Books, 2003), for a lively and informative discussion of new working conditions.

3. According to the U.S. Department of Labor, Bureau of Labor Statistics, Employment and Earnings, 2003 Household Data Annual Averages, Table 11, Employed Persons by Detailed Occupation, 47,929,000 people were in management, professional, and related occupations, of whom

> 19.9 million were in management, business, and financial operations, and
> 27.9 million were in professional and related occupations.

Additionally, 19,536,000 people were in office and administrative support occupations.

Professional specialties in health, such as nurses and doctors (6.6 million) and teachers (7.7 million), are included in the above data on professional occupations and are generally considered white collar, although they may not necessarily be "office" jobs.

4. Service occupations account for 22 million jobs according to Bureau of Labor Statistics, 2003 Averages, Table 11. Food preparation and serving-related occupations are growing fast and make up over 7 million jobs of the 22 million service jobs, while personal care and service occupations, another growing area, account for 4.2 million of the total. Sales and related occupations, which comprise 15.9 million workers, are also increasing.

5. Adapted from Roger Swardson, "In One Office, the Toll of a New Machine," *Washington Post*, September 5, 1993, pp. C1, C4.

6. The firm described here, like many other telecommunication companies in the United States and in Europe, had been a solid and steady employer up until the mid-1990s when deregulation of the phone companies took on an intensive second wave. The first wave in the United States had been in the 1980s when the old monopolistic national phone companies were broken up into smaller regional firms. In the 1990s the regionals were first bought up by larger regionals, and then under further dergulation merged with or were acquired by multinational firms. While services broadened extensively from land-line phone systems to mobile and cell phones, to Internet and cable and broadband services, the number of permanent employees dwindled. Newer, less permanent jobs have been created in smaller nonunion workplaces, usually without health benefits. It is difficult to find reliable nonindustry-generated statistics on the number of workers employed by these companies.

7. U.S. Bureau of Labor Statistics, Current Population Survey, Contingent and Alternative Employment Arrangements, Febuary 2001. As of April 2004 this was the most recent Bureau of Labor Statistics comprehensive survey of contingent work. See also Steven Hipple, "Contingent Work in the Late-

1990s," *Monthly Labor Review* 124, no. 3 (March 2001), for definitions of this emerging field.

8. Phil Patton, "The Virtual Office Becomes Reality," *New York Times*, October 28, 1993.

9. Edward Tanner, "The Paradoxical Proliferation of Paper," *Harvard Magazine* (March–April 1988): 23–26.

2. The 1950s and 1960s: The Dawn of the Computer Age

1. C. Wright Mills, *White Collar*, (New York: Oxford University Press, 1951), preface, p. x.

2. For a discussion of the transformation of factory work, see Harley Shaiken, *Work Transformed* (New York: Holt, Rinehart and Winston, 1984), and Barry Bluestone and Bennett Harrison, *The Deindustrialization of America* (New York: Basic Books, 1982).

3. Mills, *White Collar*, p. 63.

4. See, for example, Teresa Amott, *Caught in the Crisis: Women and the U.S. Economy Today* (New York: Monthly Review Press, 1993).

5. See Ellen Lupton, *Mechanical Brides: Women and Machines from Home to Office* (New York: Princeton Archictural Press, 1993), p. 43.

6. Ibid., p. 44.

7. Mary Murphree, "Brave New Office: The Changing World of the Legal Secretary," in Karen Sacks and Dorothy Remy, eds., *My Troubles Are Going to Have Trouble with Me* (New Brunswick, NJ: Rutgers University Press, 1984); see also Mary Murphree, "New Technology and Office Tradition: The Not-so-changing World of the Secre-tary," in *Computer Chips and Paper Clips*, vol. 2, ed. Heidi Hartmann et al. (Washington, D.C.: National Academy Press, 1987).

8. Barbara Garson, *The Electronic Sweatshop* (New York: Penguin Books, 1988).

9. Juliette Webster, *Office Automation: The Labour Process and Women's Work in Britain* (London: Harvester Wheatsheaf, 1993), p. 118.

10. Joan Greenbaum, *In the Name of Efficiency: Management Theory and Shopfloor Practice in Data-Processing Work* (Philadelphia: Temple University Press, 1979).

11. Ibid., p. 65.

12. Ibid., p. 64.

13. R. Boguslaw, *The New Utopians: A Study of System Design and Social Change* (Englewood Cliffs, NJ: Prentice-Hall, 1965), p. 2.

3. The 1970s: The Office as the Factory of the Future

1. U.S. Department of Health, Education, and Welfare, Special Taskforce Report, *Work in America* (Cambridge, MA: MIT Press, 1973), p. 38.

2. Daniel Bell, *The Coming of the Post-Industrial Society* (New York: Basic Books, 1976).

3. Joan Greenbaum, *In the Name of Efficiency* (Philadelphia, PA: Temple University Press, 1979), p. 29.

4. Pelle Ehn, *Work-Oriented Design of Computer Artifacts* (Hillside, NJ: Lawrence Erlbaum Associates, 1990).

5. Russell Ackoff, *Redesigning the Future: A Systems Approach to Societal Programs* (New York: Wiley, 1974), p. 8.

6. In the early 1970s, when I was a systems consultant for the Bureau of Child Welfare in New York City, I saw firsthand the effect that system design had on cutting recipients out of social services and cutting social work into parts. During this period, welfare roles were growing and government agencies were looking for new ways to cut the costs of processing and providing services. Ross Perot, for example, made a fortune by winning the contracts to process the welfare checks in most states. He claimed that his firm could do it for less. Meanwhile, in New York City in the late 1960s, social workers went on strike to try to stop the division of labor and the de-skilling that the new systems were bringing to their profession.

7. See Greenbaum, *In the Name of Efficiency*, p. 29.

8. Engineers that I have spoken to have said that an input device for handwriting with close to 90 percent accuracy would not have been likely in 1968. Since the project was secret at the time, there is no way to go back and confirm how dependable or accurate it was, but the point here is that it was certainly far enough along for marketing studies to begin, and far enough along for management to be making plans to take it "from the lab" to some practical application.

9. Richard Edwards, *Contested Terrain: The Transformation of the Workplace in the Twentieth Century* (New York: Basic Books, 1979), p. 21.

10. U.S. Department of Health, Education, and Welfare, *Work in America*, pp. 48, 44.

11. Harry Braverman, *Labor and Monopoly Capital: The Degradation of Work in the Twentieth Century* (New York: Monthly Review Press, 1974), p. 126.

12. Ibid.

13. For some much-read managements books of the period see, for example, Alfred Chandler, *Strategy and Structure* (Cambridge, MA: MIT Press, 1962); Herbert Simon, *The Shape of Automation for Men and Management* (New York: Harper & Row, 1965); and Peter F. Drucker, *Technology, Management, and Society* (New York: Harper & Row, 1974).

14. Braverman, *Labor and Monopoly Capital*, pp. 39, 37.

15. Cited in ibid., from Frederick Taylor, *Scientific Management* (New York: Harper, 1947), pp. 112–13, 119.

16. Studs Terkel, *Working* (New York: Avon, 1972), p. 139.

17. Ibid., p. 141.

18. U.S. Department of Health, Education, and Welfare, *Work in America*, p. 40.

19. To a certain extent, the same case could be made for factory work—namely that skill cannot be made into simple repetitive tasks, and that in many of

the cases where this was done, worker resistance took the steam of out managerial control.

20. Greenbaum, *In the Name of Efficiency*, p. 19.

21. See Daniel Bell, *The Coming of the Post-Industrial Society* (New York: Basic Books, 1976).

4. The 1980s: Stumbling Toward "Automated" Offices

1. In the early 1990s I went to Siberia to offer technical assistance to the coal miners' union. As my interpreter and I went from mine office to mine office in remote towns we found former mine workers sitting at the computers that had been donated to them and happily doing everything from word processing to playing games on the spreadsheet program that had been installed on the machine. I suggested that they use the spreadsheet for their union budget—to me a logical spreadsheet function—but they, of course, had no budget, nor had they ever thought about the need for one.

2. See, for example, T. Peters and R. Waterman, *In Search of Excellence: Lessons from America's Best-Run Companies* (New York: Harper & Row, 1982).

3. U.S. Office of Technology Assessment, *Automating America's Offices*, pp. 117–18; italics added.

4. *Forbes*, March 29, 1993, p. 49. It is difficult to find reliable figures on the number of PCs in use, especially since almost all the data comes from companies that make hardware and software.

5. Andrew Friedman, *Computer Systems Development: History, Organization, and Implementation* (New York: Wiley, 1989).

6. Joan Greenbaum and Morten Kyng, eds., *Design at Work: Cooperative Design of Computer Systems* (Hillsdale, NJ: Erlbaum Associates, 1991).

7. Liam Bannon, "From Human Factors to Human Actors," in ibid, Ch. 2.

8. Most Large software companies (including Microsoft) have used user-testing labs and sets of procedures in which interface changes and program features are tested in focus groups. It is rare to see software actually tested in real work environments, except fot he so-called beta versions of software, which are usually distributed to a control group of expert users to test.

9. Yourdon, *Managing the Structured Techniques* (New York: Yourdon Press, 1986), p. 61.

10. Joan Greenbaum and Morten Kyng, "Situated Design," in Greenbaum and Kyng, eds., *Design at Work*, Ch. 1.

11. Shoshana Zuboff, *In the Age of the Smart Machine* (New York: Basic Books, 1989), p. 57.

12. Barbara Garson, *Electronic Sweatshop* (New York: Penguin Books, 1988), p. 45.

13. Juliette Schor, *The Overworked American* (New York: Basic Books, 1991).

14. U.S. Office of Technology Assessment, *Automating America's Offices* (U.S. Congress, Government Printing Office, 1985), p. 27.16. See, for example,

Zuboff, *In the Age of the Smart Machine*, and Paul Adler, "New Technologies, New Skills," *California Management Review* 29, no. 1 (Fall 1986).

15. See ibid, p. 28.

16. See, for example, Zuboff, *In the Age of the Smart Machine*, and Paul Adler, "New Technologies, New Skills," *California Management Review* 29, no. 1 (Fall 1986).

17. Robert Howard, *Brave New Workplace* (New York: Viking, 1985), p. 111.

18. Ibid, p. 112.

19. 1Ibid.

20. U.S. Department of Labor, Bureau of Labor Statistics, Household Surveys, January 1983, Table 23.

21. Zuboff, *In the Age of the Smart Machine*, p. 170.

22. Sharon Szymanski, "Unrequited Skills: The Effect of Technology on Clerical Work," Ph.D. diss., New School for Social Research, 1989; available from University Microfilms, Ann Arbor, Michigan.

23. U.S. Office of Technology Assessment, *Automation of America's Offices*, p. 19.

5. The Early 1990s: Reengineering the Office

1. Quoted in Amalia Duarte, "Workers and AT&T Both Grapple with the Reality of Layoffs," *New York Times*, August 28, 1994, New Jersey Section, p. 1.

2. Ibid., see also Robert Reich, *The Work of Nations* (New York: Vintage, 1992) for Reich's analysis of economic change during this period.

3. Quoted in Louis Uchitelle, "The Rise of the Losing Class," *New York Times*, November 20, 1994, .

4. "The New World of Work," *Business Week*, Special Report, 65th Anniversary Issue, October 17, 1994, p. 86.

5. William Bridges, "The End of the Job," *Fortune*, September 19, 1994, pp. 62–74.

6. "Business Rolls the Dice," *Business Week* Special Report, October 17, 1994 p. 89.

7. George Church, "Jobs in the Age of Insecurity," *Time*, November 22, 1993, pp. 34–38.

8. The U.S. Bureau of Labor Statistics does not keep track of Customer Service Representatives as a separate job category. According to the BLS's *Occupational Outlook Handbook*, these workers are included under a number of different job descriptions, including the growing category of Information Clerks, which in 1995 included Credit Clerks and New Account Clerks.

9. See Harry Braverman, *Labor and Monopoly Capital* (New York: Monthly Review Press, 1974).

10. U.S. Bureau of Labor Statistics, Table 11, 1995. Data for persons of 'Hispanic Origin' were even more discouraging, accounting for only 4.4 percent of all managerial and professional occupations.

11. Data on declining occupations are taken from U.S. Bureau of Labor Statistics, Household Data Annual Averages, Table 11, 1990–95. It should be noted that according to the same data there were only 57,000 telephone operators counted in 2003.

12. Peter Kilborn, "Workplace Injury Is Rising and the Computer is Blamed," *New York Times*, December 16, 1989; Janice Horowitz, "Crippled by Computers" *Time*, October 12, 1992; and "A Price for Every Progress: Hazards of VDTs," Video. (New York: Labor Institute, 1988).

13. See Jonathan Bennett, "How Safe Are They?" *Microwave News*, November 1990; see also Paul Brodeur, "Annals of Radiation: The Hazards of Electromagnetic Fields," *The New Yorker*, June 12, 1989.

14. Richard Karlgaard, *Forbes ASAP*, December 7, 1992, p. 9.

15. *Business Week*, August 1, 1994, p. 14.

16. Louis Uchitelle, "New Economy Dashes Old Notions of Growth," *New York Times*, November 27, 1994.

17. Replacing employees with equipment was an oft-repeated theme in the *New York Times* and *Wall Street Journal* in 1993 and 1994. It was also featured in cover stories about jobs in *Business–Week*, October 17, 1994; *Fortune*, September 19, 1994; and *Time*, November 22, 1993.

6. The Late 1990s: Enter the Internet

1. Andrew Ross, *No-Collar* (New York: Basic Books, 2003), p. 40.

2. Quoted in Paul M. Sweezy et al, eds, "The New Economy: Myth and Reality," *Monthly Review* 52, no. 11 (April 2001), p. 3.

3. Doug Henwood, *After the New Economy* (New York: The New Press, 2003), p.2.

4. Quoted in Paul M. Sweezy, et al, "The New Economy," p. 2. Also see Greenspan speeches on the Federal Reserve Board website: www.federalreserve.gov.

5. Steven Hipple and Karen Kosanovich, "Computer and Internet Use at Work in 2001," *Monthly Labor Review* (February 2003), 26.

6. "CEOs Learn the Technology Ropes," *Business Week*, April 13, 2004, Special Report online at www.businessweek.com. It is interesting to note that while most CEOs are men, the "Computer and Internet Use at Work" report cited in n. 4 found that women were more likely to use computers and the Internet.

7. See Manuel Castells, *The Internet Galaxy: Reflections on the Internet, Business and Society* (New York: Oxford University Press, 2001). See chapters 1 and 2 for a comprehensive analysis of the history of the Internet, see also www.isoc.org/internet-history/brief.html.

8. Ibid., chapter 2.

9. David McGuire, "U.N. Sets Aside Debate Over Control of Internet," *Washington Post*, December 9, 2003.

10. See www.usdoj.gov/atr/cases for more information about the extensive Microsoft antitrust cases. See also "Coming to Grips with Microsoft," *Business Week*, November 2, 1998.

11. Paul Baran and Paul Sweezy, *Monopoly Capital* (New York: Monthly Review Press, 1966). See also Michael Dawson and John Bellamy Foster, "Virtual

Capitalism: The Political Economy of the Information Highway," *Monthly Review* 48, no. 3 (April 1996).

12. For up-to-date accounts of international multimedia firms see www.computerworld.com, and www.informationweek.com.

13. Castells, *The Internet Galaxy*, p. 28; also see Claude Fischer, *America Calling* (Berkeley, CA: University of California Press, 1992) for a history of telephone use.

14. In the interviews I conducted in 1993 and 1994 for the first edition of this book, I was surprised to find that most of the people I interviewed commented that their employers either didn't want them to use e-mail at work or tried to limit use to certain days or hours. The debate continues today with companies trying to limit use of the World Wide Web during working hours, despite the fact that many workers need it for work-related information.

15. See Howard Rheingold, *The Virtual Community: Homesteading on the Electronic Frontier* (Cambridge, MA: MIT Press, 1993).

16. U. S. Bureau of Labor Statistics, Table 11, Household Annual Averages, 1995, 2000.

17. "U.S. Government Report: IT Industry Growing Again," *Network World Fusion*, January 17, 2003. See www.nwfusion.com. The Information Technology Association of America, a trade association, claimed, however, that there were 10.4 million workers in the U.S. IT industry around the same time period. See Amy Schurr, "Demand for IT Pros Shrank in 2001," *Network World Fusion*, May 20, 2002.

18. Ramin Jaleshgari, "IT Labor Shortage Persists, Hurting the Economy," *Information Week* 757 (October 18, 1999): 34. Note that while there was a labor shortage in IT in the late 1990s, the service and support jobs were among the lowest paying jobs.

19. For a fascinating and fictional account of the software process of debugging, see Ellen Ullman, *The Bug* (New York: Nan A. Talese Books, 2003).

20. Harry Braverman, *Labor and Monopoly Capital* (New York: Monthly Review Press, 1974).

21. See *Business Week*, *Wall Street Journal*, industry websites from this period. The numbers here are also hard to pin down. According to an Information Technology Association of America (ITAA) report, the IT industry lost 500,000 jobs in 2001, but they claim that companies fired 2.6 million IT workers *and* hired 2.1 million IT workers in the same year. Schurr, "Demand for IT Pros Shrank in 2001."

22. See Ross, *No-Collar*.

23. See Bill Gates, *The Road Ahead* (New York: Viking, 1995).

24. Ibid., pp. 241–42.

25. Dawson and Foster, "Virtual Capitalism," *Monthly Review* 48, no. 3 (April 1996), p. 42.

7. The Office of the Future Is Everywhere

1. Nelson Schwartz and Ann Harrington, "Down and Out in White-Collar America," in *Fortune*, June 23, 2003, vol. 147, Issue 13, pl. 78.

2. See U. S. Bureau of Labor Statistics, www.bls.gov; and Aaron Bernstein, "One Giant Global Labor Pool," *Business Week*, March 22, 2004, online at www.businessweek.com.

3. Aaron Bernstein, "One Giant Global Labor Pool," *Business Week*, March 22, 2004, online at www.businessweek.com.

4. Pete Engardio et al., "Is your Job Next?" *Business Week*, February 3, 2003, p. 50.

5. See U.S. Bureau of Labor Statistics, "Contingent and Alternative Employment Arrangements," February 2001.

6. See Richard Edwards, *Contested Terrain: The Transformation of the Workplace in the Twentieth Century* (New York: Basic Books, 1979).

7. See Stanley Aronowitz, *The Knowledge Factory* (Boston: Beacon Press, 2000); see also Benjamin Johnson et al., *Steal this University: The Rise of the Corporate University and the Academic Labor Movement* (New York: Routledge, 2003).

8. See American Association of University Professors, www.aaup.org.

9. Scott Smallwood, "United Academic Workers," *Chronicle of Higher Education* 49, no. 19 (January 17, 2003) online at www.chronicle.com. More recent estimates at least triple this number. See also David Noble, *Digital Diploma Mills* (New York: Monthly Review Press, 2001).

10. For a good analysis and overview of U.S. social history see Howard Zinn, *A People's History of the United States* (New York: HarperCollins, 2003).

11. For a better understanding of how pervasive technological determinism is in the West, see Merritt Roe Smith and Leo Marx, eds., *Does Technology Drive History?* (Cambridge, MA: MIT Press, 1998); and Michael Adas, *Machines as the Measure of Men* (Ithaca, NY: Cornell University Press, 1989).

12. Florence Olsen, "Investments in Privately Held Distance-Education Companies Dropped in 2002," *Chronicle of Higher Education* 49, no. 34 (May 2, 2003): A40.

13. Dan Carnevale, "New School and Open U. to Collaborate," *Chronicle of Higher Education* 49, no. 22 (February 7, 2003).

14. See Scott Smallwood, "United Academic Workers," *Chronicle of Higher Education* 49, no.19 (January 17, 2003): 19. See also www.laboreducator.org.

15. David M. Gordon, *Fat and Mean, the Corporate Squeeze of Working Americans and the Myth of Managerial Downsizing* (New York: The Free Press, 1996).

16. Jill Andresky Fraser, *White Collar Sweatshop, The Deterioration of Work and Its Rewards in Corporate America* (New York: W. W. Norton, 2001), pp. 30–31.

17. See Andrew Ross Sorkin, "$58 Billion Deal to Unite 2 Giants of U. S. Banking," *New York Times*, January 15, 2004. The article reports that 10,000 jobs will be lost in this merger.

18. Andrew Ross, *No-Collar: The Humane Workplace and Its Hidden Costs* (New York: Basic Books, 2003), p. 12.

19. Fraser, *White Collar Sweatshop,* p. 85.

20. Ibid.

21. See Engardio et al., "Is your Job Next?".; see also the weekly newspaper *Computerworld* during late 2003 and early 2004 for updates on IT departments and jobs that were sent to overseas software companies.

22. See also www.afl-cio.org.

23. Thomas Hoffman, "Bank's IT Workers Threaten Strike Over Outsourcing Deal," *Computerworld* 37, no.17 (April 28, 2003): 1.

24. See Louis Uchitelle, "Incentives Lure Many to Quit, Even with a Lean Job Market," *New York Times,* January, 11, 2004. Also see U.S. Bureau of Labor Statistics, Current Population Survey data on BLS website, www.bls.gov., tables A-11, A-12, A-13.

25. David Streitfeld, "Jobless Count Skips Millions," *Los Angeles Times,* December 29, 2003, p. A1.

26. See Douglas Shuitt, "Getting the Real Numbers," *Workforce* 82, no. 5 (May 2003): 16.

27. Bureau of Labor Statistics, www.bls.gov., Current Population Survey, Table B-2, 1999; in Fraser, *White Collar Sweatshop,* p. 21.

28. Ibid. Also see BLS, "Contingent and Alternative Work Arrangements," and "Work at Home Technical Note," www.bls.gov.

29. Frasier, *White Collar Sweatshop,* chap. 1.

30. Ursula Huws, *The Making of a Cybertariat: Virtual Work in a Real World* (New York: Monthly Review Press, 2003).

31. Ibid., p.23.

32. Barbara Garson, *The Electronic Sweatshop* (New York: Penguin Books, 1988), p. 60.

33. Dolores Hayden, *The Power of Place, Urban Landscapes as Public History* (Cambridge, MA: MIT Press, 1997), p.15.

34. See Maggie Jackson, *What's Happening to Home? Balancing Work, Life, and Refuge in the Information Age* (Notre Dame, IN: Sorin Books, 2002).

35. Stephanie Armour, "Benefits in U. S. Evolving," *Arizona Republic,* December 27, 2003.

8. Shaking Off False Assumptions

1. Aaron Bernstein, "One Giant Global Labor Pool?" *Business Week,* March 22, 2004; online www.businessweek.com.

2. Software and technology development, like engineering work, is broken up into different stages. Generally one or two firms develop the specifications that detail what the system is supposed to do. Then these specifications are sent out for bids. Today, given the large nature of many of these technology projects, as well as the international nature of capitalism, the bidding is

done by companies around the world. On many large projects the international firms form consortiums, which bid together.

3. Karl Marx, *Communist Manifesto*, (New York, Monthly Review Press, 1998), p. 7.

4. Joan Greenbaum, *In the Name of Efficiency* (Philadelphia:Temple University Press, 1979).

5. Object-oriented programming was first conceived in Norway by Kristen Nygaard and Ole Johann Dal with their development of the SIMULA language for simulating models. Nygaard, distressed by management control over technology in general and programming in particular, went on to create union-based training for workers to gain a better understanding of technology. He was instrumental in leading a coalition that pushed the Norwegian parliment (and later other Scandinavian countries) to institute co-determination laws that gave workers the right to decide what type of technology they used in their work. I am deeply indebted to the memory of Kristen Nygaard for his inspiration and energy in bringing about both technical and political change.

6. The *Bureau of Labor Statistics Occupational Outlook Handbook* (www.bls.gov) has finally reshuffled and redefined computer specialist jobs categories. The data in 2002 noted that there were 979,000 computer systems analysts, database administrators, and computer scientists, broken down into the following occupational titles:

   Computer systems analysts 468,000
   Nework systems and data communication analysts 186,000
   Database administrators 110,000
   Computer and information research scientists 23,000
   Other compute specialists 192,000

   The numbers are lower than those reported by IT industry association reports, but probably reflect the distribution of jobs more accurately, although the job titles and occupational categories continue to change rapidly.

7. Kathleen Madigan,"Outsourcing Jobs: Is it bad?" *Business Week*, Special Issue, European Edition, August 18–25, 2003.

8. There is a large and growing body of books about how technology kills jobs. Jeremy Rifkin's often cited *End of Work* (New York: Putnam, 1995), is indictative of the genre that proclaims that technology is taking away jobs.

9. For some earlier management classics on the poles of management see: Peter Drucker, *The Age of Discontinuity* (New York: Harper & Row, 1969); Douglas McGregor, *The Human Side of Enterprise* (New York: McGraw Hill, 1960); and Thomas Peters and Robert Waterman, *In Search of Excellence* (New York: Harper & Row, 1982). Andrew Ross's more recent analysis of these debates and their consequences is very useful for understanding management arguments, see *No-Collar*, "The Humane Workplace and Its Hidden Costs," 2003, op. cit.

10. Michael Adas, *Machines as the Measure of Men* (Ithaca, NY: Cornell University Press, 1989). It should be noted that prior to the rise of a manufacturing industry in Europe, goods from Asia, Northern Africa and the Middle East, were considered more "advanced" and were made with technology and labor processes that did not exist in Europe at that time.

11. In Michael Yates, "Poverty and Inequality," *Monthly Review* 55, no. 9 (Febuary 2004), p. 42; originally cited in Branko Milanovic, "True World Income Distribution," *The Economic Journal*, 112 (January 2002), pp. 51–92.

12. Ibid; See also Michael Yates, *Naming the System: Inequality and Work in the Global Economy*, (New York: Monthly Review Press, 2003), p. 53.

13. Ibid; see also Paul Krugman's website www.wws.princeton.edu/~pkrugman, and Krugman, *The Great Unraveling: Losing Our Way in the New Century* (New York: W.W. Norton, 2003).

14. See, for example, Kevin Phillips, "With Inequality of Income and Tax Burden Growing, Expect the Widening Rich/Poor Divide to Focus on the Political Debate," *Los Angeles Times*, 16 April 2000.

15. In particular, the rapid destablization of the Brazilian economy in 1999 and Argentina in 2003 were marked by popular uprisings. Both economic crises were propelled by monetary demands set by the World Bank and the WTO. See *The Nation*, www.thenation.org, and Monthly Review Press, www.monthlyreview. org, for recent examples.

16. The enormous popular outpouring against the World Trade Organization in 1999 in Seattle set the stage for public discussion about the then newly emerging patterns of redivision of worldwide labor, otherwise called globalization. Since then, such demonstrations have taken place throughout the world wherever WTO and other world business leaders meet to set agendas. Not insignificantly, corporate scandals like those of Enron and Global Crossing in 2002–2003 made it clear that without public scrutiny, corporate accounting practices and large scale mergers and acquistions were rife with clearly illegal actions.

17. As discussed in the last chapters, white-collar corporate jobs were largely open to white men up through the 1980s, when women began to gain a toehold in this relatively secure workforce. While women made up 50 percent of professional and managerial jobs in 2003, only 8 percent were held by African Amercians and 6 percent by Latinos, according to the U.S. Department of Labor, Bureau of Labor Statistics, *Employment and Earnings*, 2003 Household Data Annual Averages, Table 11, Employed Persons by Detailed Occupation.

18. The civil rights struggles in the South were tightly interwoven with labor and union struggles. Martin Luther King Jr., the great civil rights leader, was continually outspoken about the need for good jobs and labor rights. See the Martin Luther King Papers project website for speeches, letters, writings: www.stanford.edu/group/King.

19. There is much written about computer hackers. An important and up-to-date source is the Electronic Frontier Foundation (www.eff.org). Europe First Monday (www.firstmonday.dk) publishes analytical articles about electronic issues, in English, and likewise the website of a noted European sometimes hacker, Gisle Hannemyr, is useful (www.folk.uio.no/gisle). Open source software is written so that the code can be shared by everyone. It is a growing and important counter-corporate control movement in the IT world.

20. Lucy Suchman, an anthropologist, has written extensively about work culture. Her website at the University of Lancaster in England links to her writing: www.comp.lancs.ac.uk/sociology/staff/suchman/suchman.htm. See also John Seely Brown and Paul Duguid, *The Social Life of Information* (Boston: Harvard Business School Press, 2000).

21. C. Wright Mills, *White Collar:The American Middle Class* (New York: Oxford, 1956).

22. Ursula Huws, *The Making of a Cybertariat* (New York: Monthly Review Press, 2003), p. 165.

23. Neil Stephenson, *Snow Crash* (New York: Bantam, 2000), p. 39.

24. In 1968, working for a subsidiary of IBM, I was offered the "opportunity" to move up to lower management. While I didn't choose that path, I was informed about IBM's anti-union policies, which were so extensive that if two or more employees came with a similar demand it should be met rather than allowing workers to get together a union. I was also told that other corporations had similar policies.

25. "Fact-Finding Report: Commission on the Future of Worker-Management Relations," the *Dunlop Report.*

Postcsript

1. Ursula Huws, *The Making of a Cybertariat: Virtual Work in a Real World* (New York: Monthly Review Press, 2003), p. 165.

Useful Resources

Books

Adas, Michael, *Machines as the Measure of Men* (Ithaca, NY: Cornell University Press, 1990).

Agree, Philip and Marc Rotenberg, eds., *Technology and Privacy: The New Landscape* (Cambridge, MA: MIT Press, 1998).

Aronowitz, Stanley, *The Knowledge Factory* (Boston, MA: Beacon Press, 2000).

————, *The Last Good Job in America* (Lanham, MD: Rowman & Littlefield, 2001).

Bell, Daniel, *The Coming of Post-Industrial Society* (New York: Basic Books, 1976).

Bluestone, Barry and Bennett Harrison, *The Deindustrialization of America* (New York: Basic Books, 1982).

Braverman, Harry, *Labor and Monopoly Capita:, The Degradation of Work in the Twentieth Century* (New York: Monthly Review Press, 1974).

Brown, John Seely, and Paul Duguid, *The Social Life of Information* (Cambridge, MA: Harvard Business School Books, 2002).

Castells, Manuel, *The Internet Galaxy: Reflections on the Internet, Business and Society* (New York: Oxford, 2001).

Castells, Manuel, *The Rise of the Network Society* (Oxford, UK: Blackwell, 1996).

Drucker, Peter, *The Age of Discontinuity* (New York: Harper & Row, 1969)

Edwards, Richard, *Contested Terrain: The Transformation of the Workplace in the Twentieth Century* (New York: Basic Books, 1979).

Fraser, Jill Andresky, *White Collar Sweatshop: The Deterioration of Work and Its Rewards in Corporate America* (New York: W.W. Norton, 2001).

Garson, Barbara, *The Electronic Sweatshop: How Computers Are Transforming the Office of the Future into the Factory of the Past* (New York: Simon and Schuster, 1988).

Giedion, Siegfried, *Mechanization Takes Command*, (Oxford, UK: Oxford University Press, 1948).

Gordon, David, *Fat and Mean: The Corporate Squeezing of Working Americans and the Myth of Managerial Downsizing* (New York: Martin Kessler, 1996).

Greenbaum, Joan, and Morton Kyng, eds., *Design at Work: Cooperative Design of Computer Systems* (Hillsdale, NJ: Erlbaum Press, 1991).

Greenbaum, Joan, *In the Name of Efficiency*, (Philadelphia: Temple University Press, 1979).

———, *Windows on the Workplace*, 1st ed. (New York: Monthly Review Press, 1995).

Hafner, Katie, and John Markoff, *Cyberpunks: Outlaws and Hackers in the Ccomputer Frontier* (New York: Touchstone, 1995).

Hayden, Dolores, *The Power of Place: Urban Landscapes as Public History* (Cambridge MA: MIT Press, 1995).

Heckscher, Charles, *White-Collar Blues: Management Loyalties in an Age of Corporate Restructuring* (New York: Basic Books, 1995).

Henwood, Doug, *After the New Economy* (New York: The New Press, 2003).

Hochschild, Arlene, *The Time Bind: When Work Becomes Home and Home Becomes Work* (New York: Metropolitan Books, 1997).

Howard, Robert, *Brave New Workplace* (New York: Viking Press, 1985).

Huws, Ursula, *The Making of a Cybertariat* (New York: Monthly Review Press, 2003).

Jackson, Maggie, *What's Happening to Home?* (Notre Dame, IN: Sorin Books, 2002).

Johnson, Benjamin et al., *Steal This University: The Rise of the Corporate University and the Academic Labor Movement* (New York: Routledge, 2003).

Jones, Steve, ed., *Cybersociety 2.0* (London: Sage, 1999).

Krugman, Paul, *The Great Unraveling: Losing Our Way in the New Century* (New York: W. W. Norton, 2003).

Lupton, Ellen, *Mechanical Brides: Women and Machines from Home to Office* (New York: Princeton Architectural Press, 1993).

Marx, Karl, *Capital, Vol. I.* (New York: Penguin, 1976).

McChesney, Robert W., *The Problem of the Media* (New York: Monthly Review Press, 2004).

McGregor, Douglas, *The Human Side of Enterprise* (New York: McGraw-Hill, 1960).

Mills, C. Wright, *White Collar, The American Middle Class* (New York: Oxford, 1956).

Montgomery, David, *Workers' Control in America* (Cambridge: Cambridge University Press, 1979).

Noble, David, *Digital Diploma Mills* (New York: Monthly Review Press, 2001).

Noble, David, *The Religion of Technology* (New York: Knopf, 1997).

Peters, Thomas and Robert Waterman, *In Search of Excellence* (New York; Harper & Row, 1982).

Postman, Neil, *Technopoly* (New York: Vintage, 1993).

Reich, Robert, *The Work of Nations* (New York: Knopf, 1991).

Rheingold, Howard, *The Virtual Community: Homesteading on the Electronic*

Frontier (Cambridge, MA: MIT Press, 1993/2000).

Rifkin, Jeremy, *The End of Work* (New York: Putnam, 1995).

Ross, Andrew, *No-Collar: The Humane Workplace and Its Hidden Costs* (New York: Basic Books, 2003).

Schiller, Dan, *Digital Capitalism: Networking the Global Market System* (Cambridge, Mass: MIT Press, 1999).

Schor, Juliette, *The Overworked American* (New York: Basic Books, 1991).

Sennett, Richard, *The Corrosion of Character: The Personal Consequences of Work in the New Capitalism* (New York: W. W. Norton, 1998).

Shaiken, Harley, *Work Transformed* (New York: Holt, Rinehart and Winston, 1984).

Smith, Merritt Roe. and Leo Marx, eds., *Does Technology Drive History* (Cambridge, MA: MIT Press, 1998).

Suchman, Lucy, *Plans and Situated Actions: Problems of Human-Machine* Communication (New York: Cambridge University Press, 1987).

Sweezy, Paul, and Paul Baran, *Monopoly Capital* (New York: Monthly Review Press, 1966).

Terkel, Studs, *Working,* (New York: Pantheon, 1974).

Thompson, Paul and Chris Warhurst, eds., *Workplaces of the Future* (London: Macmillan, 1998).

Turkle, Sherry, *Life on the Screen: Identity in the Age of the Internet* (New York: Simon and Schuster, 1995).

Whyte, William, *The Organization Man,* (New York: Simon and Schuster, 1956).

Yates, Michael D,. *Naming the System: Inequality and Work in the Global Economy* (New York: Monthly Review Press, 2003).

Zuboff, Shoshana, *In the Age of the Smart Machine* (New York: Basic Books, 1989).

Websites

American Federation of Labor: www.afl-cio.org

Brecher, Jeremy, "Outsource This!": www.fairjobs.org/docs/OutsourceThis!.pdf

Business Week magazine, weekly: www.businessweek.com..

Computer World magazine, weekly: www.computerworld.com.

Electronic Frontier Foundation: www.eff.org

Economic Policy Institute: www.epinet.org/content.cfm/datazone_index

Information Week magazine, weekly: www.informationweek.com.

International Labor Organization: www.ilo.org.

Internet Archives: www.archive.org.

Institute for Policy Studies: www.ips-dc.org.

Paul Krugman, articles and columns: www.wws.princeton.edu/~pkrugman.

World Bank: www.Worldbank.org.

The Nation magazine, weekly: www.thenation.org

U. S. Department of Labor, Bureau of Labor Statistics: www.bls.gov.

Wired magazine: www.wired.com.

Index